Help Your Child

Homework and Exams

A PARENTS' HANDBOOK

Jennie Lindon

Hodder & Stoughton

A MEMBER OF THE HODDER HEADLINE GROUP

*To my mother and father
who helped me so much with my schoolwork*

Cataloguing in Publication Data is available from the British Library

ISBN 0 340 658665

First published 1996
Impression number   10 9 8 7 6 5 4 3
Year   1999 1998 1997

Copyright © 1996 Jennie Lindon

All rights reserved. No part of this publication may be reproduced or transmitted in any form or by any means, electronic or mechanical, including photocopy, recording, or any information storage and retrieval system, without permission in writing from the publisher or under licence from the Copyright Licensing Agency Limited. Further details of such licences (for reprographic reproduction) may be obtained from the Copyright Licensing Agency Limited, of 90 Tottenham Court Road, London, W1P 9HE.

Typeset by Wearset, Boldon, Tyne and Wear
Printed in Great Britain for Hodder & Stoughton Educational, a division of Hodder Headline Plc, 338 Euston Road, London NW1 3BH by Cox & Wyman Ltd, Reading, Berks.

Contents

1 **Studying at home**   Parents can help. Working well with your child's school. Building your child's confidence   5

2 **Good standards in homework**   Doing what is asked. Effective essay writing. Checking work. Reading and making notes. The use of diagrams.   27

3 **Homework for different subjects**   English (or Welsh) as a first language. Foreign languages. Maths. Science. Practical subjects. Preparing to speak in class. Difficulties with a subject.   47

4 **Preparing for tests and exams**   Helping with class tests. Revision for exams. Preparing for orals.   74

5 **Sitting exams**   Worries about exams. Effective exam techniques. Different kinds of questions. Writing good answers. Exam and test results.   92

6 **GCSE coursework and exams**   The GCSE programme. Producing good coursework. The marking of coursework. Revision for GCSEs. Experience of papers. The GCSE exam period. The results.   110

Index   140

Acknowledgements

I am grateful to the many parents, children and young people who have shared their experiences and opinions on homework and exams. I would like to thank my family – Lance, Drew and Tanith Lindon for their comments and ideas.

Thank you to Tanith and Drew, Cathy Darlington, Maddie Johnston and Zoe Wheeler for helping with the handwritten examples in the book. Chapter 6 benefited from the suggestions of Innes Johnston, Miriam Turner and Nancy Wheeler.

During the summer term of 1995, three schools arranged for me to run informal discussions with children and teenagers across the age range from Year 5 to the sixth form. I would like to thank the teachers and pupils of Ravenstone Primary School, The Angmering School and Burntwood School.

The publishers would like to thank the children of Charlbury Primary School, Oxfordshire, for their help with the covers for this series.

CHAPTER ONE

Studying at home

Parents can help

Parents vary in their attitudes towards helping with homework, or with revision for exams. Some see this involvement as a natural part of being a parent. However, some parents are very capable in their own working lives but remain uncertain about whether they should help with their children's homework or their revision for exams. This section covers questions that are often asked by parents.

Isn't it cheating to help my child?

The simple answer is, "No". You are supporting him and helping him to learn if you follow the kinds of approaches that are given in this book. Children learn from their teachers, from each other and from a wide range of materials. They are not expected to work only with the resources inside their own heads. You would be dishonest if you did a great deal of the work for your child and he submitted it as his unaided efforts.

What if I don't understand the subject either?

Part of learning is understanding how to find something out when you do not know, or how to make a best guess from what you do understand. Your child will not think any the less of you for not knowing and will appreciate your efforts to problem-solve with her.

Schools have changed since I was a child

There has undoubtedly been a great deal of change, not only in the curriculum itself, but in teaching methods and the way that children are assessed. But none of these changes means that parents are disqualified from helping.

Some changes are a positive help to parents as they support their children. Workbooks, which have manageable chunks of text and are generously illustrated, have largely taken over from textbooks. As a parent, you will be able to get a basic understanding of a topic far quicker by looking at a double page spread of your child's workbook than by trying to speed-read pages of text.

Supposing I give them the wrong answer?

There is always the possibility that parents may feel very sure and yet turn out to be wrong on an answer or the best approach to a piece of homework. Your best bet as a helpful parent is to admit if you do not know, work with your child to find the most likely answer or the best way to approach tonight's homework. If you do turn out to be confident, but wrong, then apologise and see what you, and your child can learn from the mistake. You have far more chance of a friendly outcome with your child if you show that adults are not invariably right.

It is not always the best idea to hand over a correct answer immediately to your child. It is far better to help him to find his

STUDYING AT HOME

own way to the answer, or generate his own ideas rather than just pick your brains. Many suggestions are given throughout this book to help with this.

Surely the teachers will think I'm interfering

No. Good teachers will be delighted that you are supporting your child, and therefore the work of the school, from home. Most schools have abandoned the stance of several decades ago that parents knew little and teachers were the only ones who understood education. You will find that some teachers are more approachable and positive towards parents than others, but every profession has this variability.

I don't have the time to help

Helping your child with homework does not mean sitting with him for the entire time that he is completing his homework every day. He would probably find that very intrusive and hovering over him will not encourage your child in the confidence of independent study. Effective help from a parent is much more about being available to be asked for help and trying hard to give time when it is requested. If you cannot offer help immediately give a clear promise about when you will be able to help and stick to it – delays in help may discourage your child from asking. Helping also involves showing interest and taking the time to look at your child's work.

Depending on your commitments, including your paid work, you may need to come to a compromise with your child about when (in the evening or at the weekend) he does his homework, so that you are at home and can stop what you are doing to help. Different households have to find their own way over timing, as well as which parent will help in a two-parent household.

Working well with your child's school

Good communication from schools

You will be far more able to help and support your child if her school gives you sufficient information and keeps the lines of communication open. Schools have slightly different ways of achieving good communication with parents but they should all make a serious effort.

Homework charters and marking policy

Some schools provide written information about the school policy on homework and the likely amounts for each year. A similar booklet may also explain the system of marking and grades used in the school. It can be easier for parents when all the relevant information is summarised in this way, but teachers should be very willing to answer your questions in conversation.

Homework timetables and diaries

It will help you to know the Year's timetable of subjects and which give homework on what night, and how much. Some schools provide a homework diary in which pupils write their assignments for each day. There is space for parents to sign, usually at the end of each week, to show that the homework has been completed. Some have space for you to write brief comments.

Marking and constructive comment

Teachers have an obligation to mark your child's work promptly. Work is not going to be turned around within a day, but the time should not stretch into weeks. Some schools make specific commitments in their own charters on how swiftly homework will be marked and given back to pupils. Children also need and deserve useful comments and criticisms on work done both in the classroom and at home. Teachers do not have the time to write paragraphs on each exercise book, but, it is fair to expect some encouraging comments and for critical remarks to give some indication on how your child can improve.

Easy contact with teachers

Parents need to have straightforward access to teachers. It would not be reasonable to charge into school and demand to see a particular teacher immediately. However, a courteous approach over the telephone or by letter should bring a prompt reply. Some schools like parents to use the homework diary as a first step in communications. Teachers will then make an appointment for a parent to come into school to discuss any concerns.

Some schools help parents by sending a letter in Year 7, and sometimes in subsequent Years, to explain which teacher should be the first point of contact. Schools organise themselves in different ways. Some like parents to go through the form or specific subject teacher in the first instance, some suggest a Year Curriculum Coordinator or Head of Year.

Schools should also arrange open evenings at least once a year for parents to meet their child's form teacher and any subject teachers. These occasions are for you to gain an overall verbal report on your child. The evening may be timed to link with a full written progress report. You are definitely not going to the evening to deal only with problems or difficulties. The evening should also be an opportunity to hear about how well your child is progressing in some subjects.

Written reports on your child

Schools are obligated to produce informative reports on your child's progress. The government Parents' Charter for education commits schools to a report at least once a year. However, parents really need some progress report on a termly basis, even if it is much briefer than the annual one.

Information to help parents to plan ahead

Parents need to have timely information about internal school exams or else they cannot offer effective help with revision. Schools know well in advance about the timing of the SATs for Year 9 or the GCSE timetable for Year 11.

Curriculum topics

Schools know exactly what has to be covered for each Year and some general information can help you to look out for useful visits you might make with your child, or for relevant television programmes and books. Some schools publish detailed curriculum guides whereas others leave it mainly up to pupils to tell their parents what topics are being covered.

A time for study

Helping children to manage their time

Part of getting used to homework is learning to organise the time available. Some children find homework a terrible blight on their social life. Others fit the obligations into their lives with less pain. But all children will need support from parents as they adjust to a school life that extends beyond the official hours of school attendance. If your child's primary school gave regular homework, the adjustment may be less of a burden.

STUDYING AT HOME

Checking up on homework

You have to keep a close eye on what homework your child has each day and how she has completed it until you are sure of her. Children do not necessarily lie, but much like adults, they can conveniently forget or convince themselves that a piece of homework will take hardly any time at all.

It is wise to have a look at your child's homework diary and not to take at face value "I haven't got any homework" until you are confident he is checking properly himself. You can ask courteously and not give the impression that you think your child is untrustworthy.

Managing a social life

Children do not have to give up their friends but they have to find time to do homework properly. You need to decide with your child whether her social time has to be after homework is completed, or whether she can be trusted to go and play for a while and come back at an agreed time. Broken commitments from your child should lead to withdrawal of playing privileges on school nights. Social events will have to be restricted to the weekend.

It is not possible for your child to maintain a very busy social schedule *and* keep up a good standard in homework. It may be feasible to organise one homework-free night – homework often does not have to be given in the very next day – but your child will not be able to postpone doing homework for several nights or rush off a skimpy piece of work without getting into trouble.

Sometimes children are confident that they can do their homework with their friend, at one of the two homes. You can only discover if this is possible by letting them try and then taking a good look at the homework afterwards. Some friends can and do work in each other's company. Others mean to work but distract each other hopelessly.

HELP YOUR CHILD WITH HOMEWORK AND EXAMS

Homework diary.

Monday
½ hour Maths workbook — By Tuesday
English essay – in rough, draft — Tomorrow
"Something I feel strongly about

Tuesday
Science – copy out and fill in table (page 23) on uses of different rocks. — By Friday.
R. Studies – read pages 10-12 of workbook finish drawing from class. — By next Tuesday.

Wednesday
French test – words on clothes, Section A2. — By Friday.
History – Essay into best. — Next Monday.

Figure 1 Extract from a homework diary

Extra-curricular commitments

Your child may have weekly activities such as Scouts or Swimming Club that are separate from her school. However, some schools offer a rich array of after-school activities: team games, music lessons or extra language work.

STUDYING AT HOME

School societies such as choir or drama club can become very time-consuming when a special production is planned. Teachers will be understandably absorbed in their own subject and they may overlook the consequences for pupils. Parents are the only people in a position to help their children keep a balance between all their obligations.

It will be you, and not the music teacher, who has to deal with a stressed son, worn out by choir rehearsals, who has still not completed his science homework. Under these circumstances, you will probably have to speak with the music teacher and discuss what compromises are possible. Even the most enthusiastic teacher should listen to a parent who is showing concern for a son or daughter's overall educational progress.

Getting down to homework

There is no doubt that the only way your child can finish a piece of homework is by getting started in the first place. What counts is not how much time was spent staring at a piece of homework but how effectively that time was used. A daughter who spends an hour playing with the cat, nibbling biscuits and keeping half an eye on the television is not going to have completed much work even if the books are all laid out neatly. Her brother may have spent only half an hour on homework but, if that has been concentrated work, then the difference in quality will show.

If your child keeps on postponing homework, then time will get genuinely tight and the worry will then get in the way of good work. It probably will not help simply to nag, as tempting as that can be. Sit down with your child and talk through the problem and what the possibilities seem to be. You might ask your child:

- What is the best time for you to do your homework?
- What will help you to get started?
- Do you want me to tell you when it is the agreed time to start homework?
- Would you be happier with some company?

You might be able to offer a compromise of reorganising your time. Perhaps he can work on the kitchen table while you are busy. If you work from an office at home, can you make him some space in the same room? Is there something domestic you could move to homework time so that you are occupied but can be interrupted? (I used the interminable ironing pile in this way.)

Do bear in mind that it is only fair that you do not cause the interruptions to your child's concentration on homework. This may mean thinking twice about insisting that it is, "About time you tidied up your bedroom" or asking him to keep an eye on a younger brother or sister.

Using a wide range of resources

Children and teenagers are encouraged by schools to consult resources beyond the subject workbook and some of this broader study will be possible from home.

General reading

You will help your child in general, not just with her English, if you can encourage her to read for pleasure and interest. Some children find great difficulty in seeing any enjoyment in reading, and these are not just children who have specific learning difficulties.

Children are more likely to read for pleasure, if they have been encouraged to take an interest in books from an early age – but there is no need to give up with older children. Here are some helpful pointers:

- Children are more likely to read if they see that you enjoy reading and there are books on the shelves at home.
- Be prepared to borrow books from the library on any topic in

STUDYING AT HOME

which your child shows an interest and to buy some, when you can.
- Your child may be more interested to try a book that has been serialised on television or turned into a film.
- It is very unwise to insist that a child reads only classics. Nowadays there is such a wide range of good books for children and teenagers that there will be something somewhere that engages his interest.
- A possibility is to see if your child would read magazines that cater to his hobbies or interests. Children who are very keen on a sport or on computer games will sometimes pore over a magazine.
- If your child wants you to share something that has caught his attention, then do your best to make the time, whether this is reading a short article or a book. You can have a conversation later.

Reference books

Your child's school should be providing all the necessary workbooks for each subject. However, some basic reference books will help at home:

- A dictionary – you can get good pocket dictionaries that will meet your child's needs, and which will not be too bulky for carrying to and from school.
- A thesaurus is useful for finding alternatives to words, since it is organised to give words that share the same meaning. You can buy a pocket thesaurus rather than a full size version. It is worth checking that the thesaurus you buy is organised in alphabetical order. The full-sized *Roget's Thesaurus* has a way of organising the material that I personally find very odd.
- A bilingual dictionary for the foreign language(s) that your child is studying. Your child's workbook should have an index

at the back, but soon it will not have all the words that he wishes to know.
- A recent atlas.

Older reference books

You may have books or reference part-works left over from your own childhood. These can still be a very useful source of information, so long as you and your child approach the material with some caution:

- The science basic material may be fine but remember that there have been many discoveries since your childhood.
- Maps for use in geography will be dated. Many countries have changed their names and borders have been re-drawn. Discussion and information about geographical features may still be very useful.
- Historical material may be accurate on facts but will be presented with the perspective of a different generation. However, children are taught now to assess source material in an objective way. The approach of a 1960s reference book to, for instance, the slave trade, can be of interest in its own right.

Using libraries

Your child should be able to borrow from the school library and from your local public library. Through using a library he will gain confidence in using the resources available:

- He needs to familiarise herself with the system of classification in the library so that he has some idea of where to look.
- Libraries will have a record of the books in stock, most likely on a computer.
- Librarians are usually very helpful and will advise a child or teenager who is searching for a particular book or material on a topic.

- Libraries often have tapes as well as books and will probably have books in different languages.
- Public libraries have reference books that cannot be borrowed but can be consulted in the library.
- Try to get your child into the habit of making useful notes when referring to books.
- Public libraries will track down books that are out on loan or available at other libraries in the area. They will also buy a book for the library that is likely to be of general use. (They may make a charge for these services, but it should not be high.)
- Public libraries may have special collections, perhaps of local interest, that can be consulted.

Magazines and newspapers

Your child may read some magazines or flick through some of the newspaper but it is more likely to be you who sees an article or news item that could be useful for your child's current topic. Perhaps she is doing a project on the Channel Tunnel and you notice an item in your daily newspaper. You could cut out the item, write the name of the newspaper and the date at the top and give it to your child. It is then up to him how he uses the material. Your child will learn that newspaper or television features are selective in their choice of material and usually have a particular approach to an event.

Television and radio programmes

Television and radio can be a source of excellent programmes that extend your child's general knowledge, and will sometimes link into his current topics at school. It is worth looking ahead in the programme guide for useful programmes. Sometimes an interesting feature will be on at an awkward time and could be recorded. A further advantage of video- or tape-recording is that making notes is far easier if the tape can be stopped or rewound. If at all possible, watch the programme with your child. He may like the company, but also you will learn more about the topic that he is covering.

Family activities

Your child will have school trips but families can also enjoy outings to:

- Museums
- Special exhibitions
- Historical houses and grounds
- Art galleries
- The cinema
- The theatre

When you are making a choice, you could decide on a visit to link in with your child's current topic at school. However, it would be unwise to organise all family outings around the curriculum – your child would feel that he can never escape from school.

Any kind of outing is that much more enjoyable and useful when you talk about what you see with your child. You will not enjoy every film or play but you can have an enjoyable discussion about what worked well in a theatrical production or the reasons why a film was so boring. Such conversations only continue so long as you are both interested to talk; a discussion becomes tedious if it is carried on endlessly.

Computers at home

If you already have a computer at home, then you will be looking at how your child might use the facilities for her homework. There is no need to buy the same software that is available at your child's school. Nor do you need to restrict yourself to programs

STUDYING AT HOME

that are labelled as "educational software". Children are most likely to use the following kinds of software for homework:

- Word processing for reports and essays.
- Graphics for drawing.
- Spreadsheets for tables or graphs.

The cost of computers (the hardware) and the programs you run on them (the software) have fallen as technology has advanced. However, computers can still be an impossible item for a family on a tight budget. No parent should feel compelled to find the money to buy or rent a home computer. Secondary schools have to provide computers and teach all pupils Information Technology.

If you decide to buy

You are more likely to end up with a useful piece of equipment if you take time to gather your information and make sure that you see a computer, its printer and any software in action. Salespeople in computer stores may be helpful, but can be incomprehensible to the first time buyer. Computer magazines may help and it is well worth talking with friends who already have a computer. Other good sources of advice when buying and using computers are:

- *The National Council for Educational Technology* which offers advice and information to anyone interested in computers and education – parents, teachers, school governors. They can be contacted at Milburn Hill Road, Science Park, Coventry CV4 7JJ. Tel: 01203 416994 and ask for the information desk.
- *The Parents' Information Network* (PIN) at Gibbs Home, Kennel Ride, Ascot, Berks, SL5 7NT. Or telephone the Helpline on 0990 134 734. Parents can join PIN for free and receive information leaflets and newsletters about children and computing.
- Send for *Help your child with computers at home* from

Ultralab, Anglia Polytechnic University, Sawyers Hall Lane, Brentwood, Essex CM15 9BT. Tel: 01277 200587. (The booklet cost £3.50 in 1995.)

Using a home computer

It is preferable to set up your computer in a shared room in the home and not in a child's bedroom. You want to be able to show an interest in your child's homework and this is less likely if the machine is tucked away behind a closed door. If you are ill at ease with computers then your chances of becoming more familiar will be very low. It is too tempting to think, "It's all beyond me. The kids know what to do." Computers that are set up in an older child's bedroom are not then available to younger children as they come to want access. Your computer may also have an array of games and you will not know how much time your child is spending on play rather than homework if the computer is installed out of your immediate sight.

The options for homework

Not all homework is suitable for transferring to the computer, of course. Answers to a maths workbook will have to be entered in your child's exercise book. Some teachers may want a project written entirely in the course folder or file. And any work that your child is doing both at school and at home may have to be written.

However, that leaves topics that your child completes entirely at home, project work and information gathering that he types into a neat version. Some GCSE coursework can be written on the word processor, although it is likely that teachers will want some handwritten material. If your home computer can handle graphs or tables, then some project work involving data can be transferred to the computer.

One objective of the National Curriculum is that Information Technology should be used in most, possibly all school subjects.

STUDYING AT HOME

So, your child's teachers should be pleased he is learning that computers are not just for IT lessons.

More expensive computers come equipped with a CD-Rom drive and it is then possible to buy a wide range of other information resources on disk, such as an encyclopaedia or an atlas. If such a computer is within your budget, you can bring the resources of entire libraries to your child's fingertips and the better software features animation, video clips and stereo sound.

Becoming familiar with the home computer

With a word processing package your child can correct the typed material on the screen with no trace of mistakes. This facility can be a great relief to children who can revise their drafts without the burden of re-copying each time. Children can move words and entire paragraphs around on the page. They also have choices over typestyle and features such as underlining or emboldening. If you get a word processing package with a spell checker, then the chore of checking for spelling mistakes is reduced. However, you still have to look out for correctly spelled words that have been used wrongly.

The possibilities of word processing outshine even a sophisticated electric typewriter but the program does not actually do the typing for you. If children are to feel positively about using the computer for projects, then they need to have gained reasonable typing skills. So, encourage your children to type, with all their fingers, on writing other than homework. It might be copying out a passage from a favourite book, a poem, something amusing that they would like to stick up in their room – anything to provide some practice.

Sitting down with your child and explaining how to use the different programs is time well spent. Children will get the best out of using graphics or spreadsheet software if they are not trying to understand the particular package at the same time as producing homework to a time deadline. Virtually all packages have an on-screen help system, which can be easier to consult than a manual.

If you are not accustomed to using a computer, a secondary school-aged son or daughter will have a headstart on you. It is then definitely worth encouraging your child to share some knowledge, and for you to assign time to practise.

Building your child's confidence

Positive criticism

This suggestion may sound like a contradiction, but it is possible to be constructive when giving ideas for improvement. Try to be specific about the homework at hand. It can be very discouraging to be told that "You're always so messy", or "You never check the spelling", because the criticism is all-encompassing. It is better to say "I can't read this bit" or "I would take another look at your spelling if I were you". These comments may not be entirely welcome, because perhaps your child really does not want to read the essay through again. But, he is far less likely to feel that you are criticising all her work.

If possible, try to offer a blend of positive and negative suggestions. It is very tempting for adults to focus all their comments on what is wrong with a piece of work and on what could be improved. Teachers sometimes make this mistake as much as parents. Children and teenagers want and deserve compliments on what they have done well and how they have improved their work. So, it is encouraging for your child if you always look for something to praise in his homework and do not make all your comments about mistakes. Likewise, be sure to say something when you notice that her spelling is more careful – even if there is still some way to go before he takes as much care as is needed.

STUDYING AT HOME

Be constructive about mistakes. Adults sometimes say "We all learn by our mistakes" but this cliché can be true only if those adults react in a helpful way. Mistakes can be opportunities to learn if they are treated as such, and not as evidence that a child is "stupid" or "careless". For example:

- What went wrong with the class test then? Do you understand now?
- Where did you start to get lost? Let's go back to the last thing you're sure you understand.
- Let's look first at how much of this is right – rather than how much is wrong.
- It must have been frustrating when the experiment went wrong. What can you learn for next time?
- I can understand that you are very disappointed in that mark. Can you see what you would have to do to get a better mark?

You want your child to have a sense of confidence so that not knowing something or making a mistake in his work is not the end of the world. It is possible to learn from most mistakes in school work and to find satisfaction in working out how the confusion arose. If you can encourage your child to take this approach, rather than to forget about or try to cover up mistakes, then you will be giving her a strong basis for study. Children whose mistakes are met with ridicule or lack of help can be far more worried about avoiding failure in their work than any thrill of possible success.

When children's confidence is low

Nothing eats away at confidence like discouragement. Children can come to have a very poor opinion of themselves if adults have focused only on mistakes, passing over successes as if they were only what a child should be doing anyway. But sometimes parents can have worked hard to boost their children's confidence, only to

HELP YOUR CHILD WITH HOMEWORK AND EXAMS

have much of the hard work undone by a bad experience at school.

For instance:

- He may be generalising from serious difficulties in one subject to a view that "I'll never be any good at school." You will need to help him as much as possible in that subject and to draw his attention to the good work he does in other subjects.
- Perhaps a crass teacher in primary school has made your child doubt himself. Parents should be supportive of school, but not to the point of pretending a bad teacher was a good one. You can be honest in your opinion, perhaps that the teacher was unfair or hopeless at explaining to your child. Your child will realise very well by now that teachers, like any group, are a mixed bunch.
- Your child may have been ground down by a scathing older brother or sister – or a younger one. It is a parent's job under these circumstances to deal with the sibling, pointing out firmly that this behaviour is cruel and that it is going to stop *now*.
- Perhaps, with hindsight, you realise that you have been too hard on your child. What seemed to you like constructive criticism was too negative. If you have two or more children, you may also find that one is more upset by criticism, however well expressed, than a brother or sister. You may need to apologise and ensure that you make at least three compliments about every piece of work that your child lets you see.
- Perhaps your child feels undermined through rivalry with a friend who seems to be doing better. You need to help your child to establish his own individuality. If his friend is actually doing better in one or more subjects then be pleased for him but reassure your child that you help him in terms of his capabilities. You are not wanting to turn him into the friend. If the

STUDYING AT HOME

friend, or a classmate, seems to have some good ideas about a subject then can your child learn from the friend?

Breaking a negative spiral

Unfortunately, children whose confidence is shaky can find it hard to put in extra effort or to be motivated by the possibility of improvement. You need to encourage your child towards "I'll have a go" rather than "I can't – it's all hopeless".

- If your child dismisses his efforts with "I'm always so stupid about science" you might counter this with "No, you're not stupid. It's just that you're having difficulty with this bit. It's a tough workbook."
- "I'll never be able to ..." may need to be nudged by your comment "I can see you're having a hard time at the moment ..." or "I know you don't understand this yet ..." Your child's attitude of "I'm hopeless at Spanish" needs to be moved towards an outlook with possibilities of "Spanish doesn't come easily to me. I have to work harder before I understand."
- When children feel very low about their abilities, it can be important for parents to recall positive moments for them. This may be reminding your son, struggling with tonight's chemistry, how he overcame difficulties in this subject last month. Your support is "How can I help you tonight?"

Over-confidence?

Some parents fear that their child has a problem with over-confidence. Perhaps you are concerned that your child is unrealistically optimistic that he need not rewrite what looks to you like a short and messy history essay. Perhaps you offer to test him on French vocabulary and he is sure there is no need to revise for the end of section test.

If the marks are good, then perhaps your child is fully justified in his confidence. If he returns disheartened or complaining about how unfair the teacher has been, then you will need to talk to him sensitively avoiding any crowing of "What did I say? But would you listen!" The most that a parent can reasonably say under these circumstance is, "I was doubtful about that essay. What did your teacher suggest?" or "Would you let me help you with your French next time?"

If you remain alert to what your child is doing in homework from the beginning of secondary school, then you have time to stand back and let him take a risk. The teacher's red pen on his history essay or a very disappointing French grade will not blight his entire school career, but it may encourage him to let you help next time. That said, do not be tempted to take over but still give him plenty of space for decisions or some calculated risks on what is, after all, his homework and not yours.

CHAPTER TWO

Good standards in homework

Doing what is asked

The first step in aiming for a good standard of work is ensuring that children know what they are supposed to do for their homework and that they complete the brief they have been given. Children need to:

- Listen to what teachers ask them to do for their homework.
- Write down the instructions clearly.
- File the worksheet or bring home the necessary books.
- Consult their notes or their homework diary when they settle to the work.
- Telephone friends in their class if they are uncertain about details of tonight's homework for a particular subject.

> ### *The power of the telephone*
>
> Telephones are extremely useful machines for finding the answer to questions like, "How many pages did we have to finish in the maths workbook?" or "Did she say it had to be in rough or best?"
>
> It is a practical step for your son or daughter to get the telephone numbers of friends in their class or set. You may have to watch that queries about homework do not extend into lengthy conversations. This risk seems to be greater with daughters than with sons, since girls' friendships are usually more conversation-orientated than boys'.

Good presentation

Rough first drafts

Some of your child's homework will be done in rough first of all. In some subjects she may have two exercise books – "rough" and "best". The following points are less crucial for rough work but your child does need to write clearly enough so that she can read what she scribbled earlier. It is also a good idea for her to start to use paragraphs and good punctuation as a matter of course. An interim step can be to add these to her rough work after she has drafted it and to mark in, perhaps with a double slash //, where his paragraph breaks will go. These improvements are then incorporated into the best version.

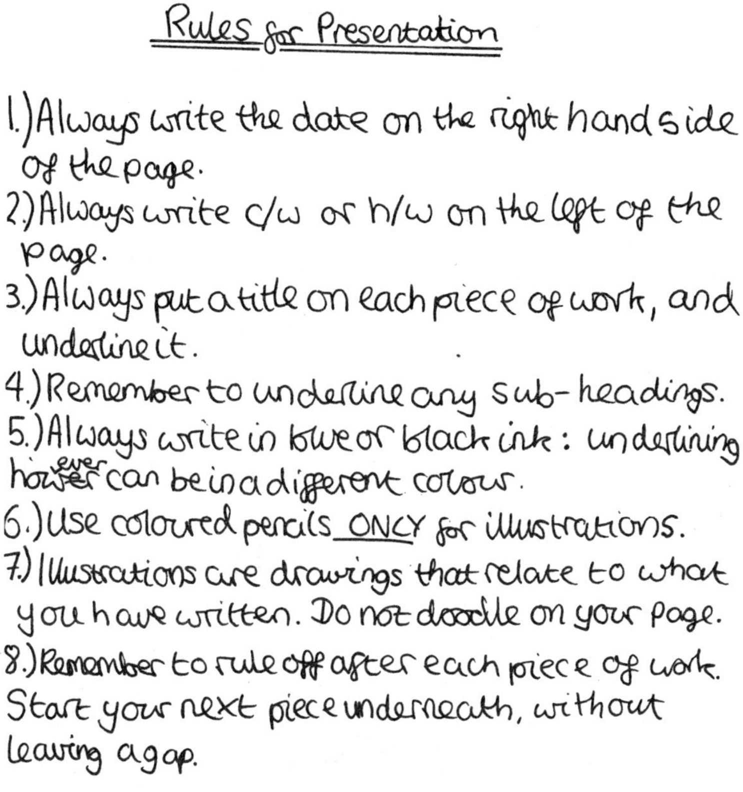

GOOD STANDARDS IN HOMEWORK

Rules for Presentation

1.) Always write the date on the right hand side of the page.
2.) Always write c/w or h/w on the left of the page.
3.) Always put a title on each piece of work, and underline it.
4.) Remember to underline any sub-headings.
5.) Always write in blue or black ink: underlining however can be in a different colour.
6.) Use coloured pencils ONLY for illustrations.
7.) Illustrations are drawings that relate to what you have written. Do not doodle on your page.
8.) Remember to rule off after each piece of work. Start your next piece underneath, without leaving a gap.

Figure 2 Teachers may provide useful rules for presentation

A word processing package on a personal computer makes the correction of first drafts a much easier task. However, to make the most of this facility, your child needs to be confident with a keyboard and to have become accustomed to working directly onto the screen. These abilities develop, but only with practice.

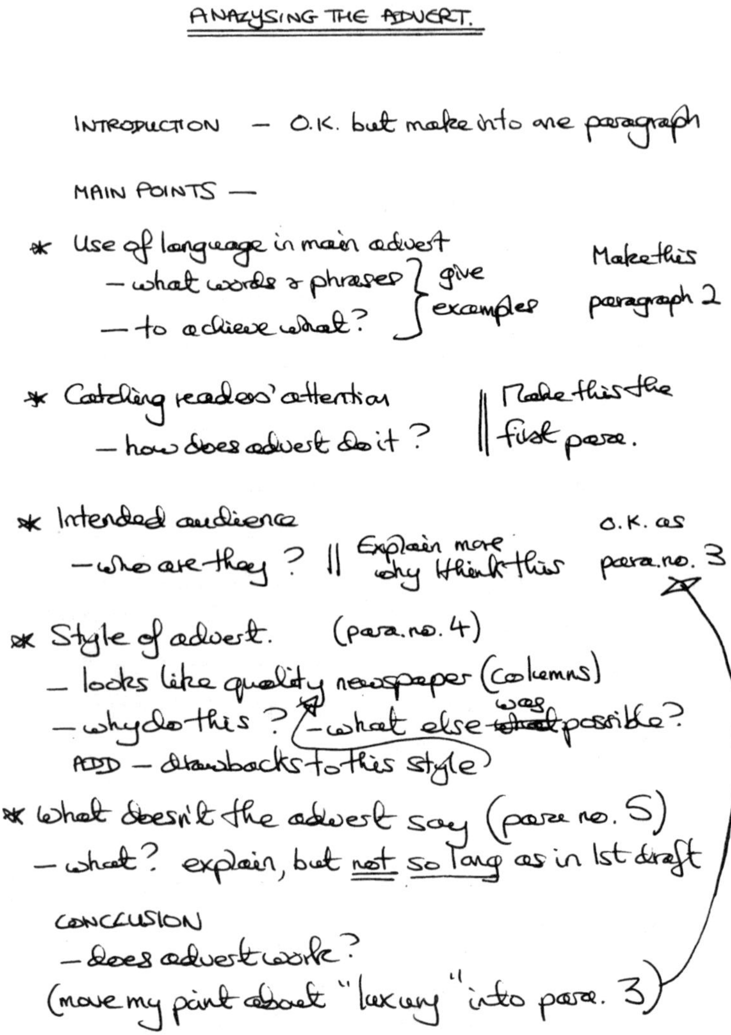

HELP YOUR CHILD WITH HOMEWORK AND EXAMS

<u>ANALYSING THE ADVERT.</u>

INTRODUCTION — O.K. but make into one paragraph

MAIN POINTS —

* Use of language in main advert — Make this
  - what words & phrases } give   paragraph 2
  - to achieve what?   } examples

* Catching readers' attention | Make this the
  - how does advert do it? | first para.

* Intended audience   O.K. as
  - who are they? || Explain more   para. no. 3
                     why I think this

* Style of advert. (para. no. 4)
  - looks like quality newspaper (columns)
  - why do this? — what else was possible?
  ADD — drawbacks to this style

* What doesn't the advert say (para no. 5)
  - what? explain, but <u>not</u> so long as in 1st draft

CONCLUSION
  - Does advert work?
  (move my point about "luxury" into para. 3)

Figure 3 Reworking a first draft

GOOD STANDARDS IN HOMEWORK

Legible writing

Schools are unlikely to insist on a standard form of handwriting and children will be allowed to develop a personal style. However, teachers need to be able to read your child's work without serious eye strain. The words need to be spaced out and the letters clearly written, otherwise, your child may be making a good point but the teacher cannot read it, or else your child's spelling might be corrected when the original was right. Your child may be able to improve her writing with your encouragement. Improved marks for work will motivate her, as will the disappearance of previously written comments from teachers like "Messy!"

Neatness is not only an issue with words. Similar problems can arise with numbers and symbols in maths or science. Scrawled

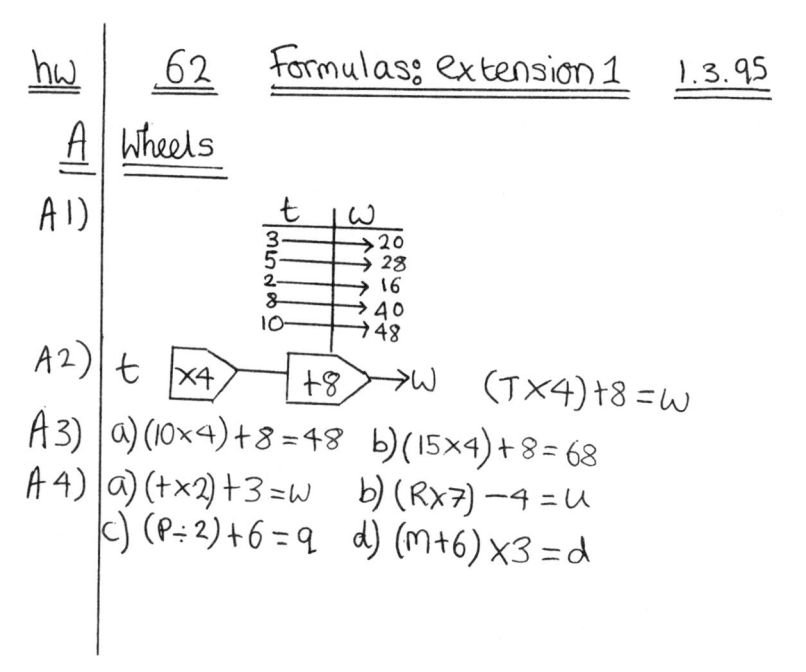

Figure 4 Example of a neat layout for maths

calculations or formulas can prove impossible for teachers to unravel.

Concentration

Sometimes children's writing causes problems simply because they do not take care. They try to complete the homework too fast or with distractions such as watching a television programme at the same time. If this is the case, they need to be encouraged to take more time over their presentation. Negotiations may also have to be reached about watching television during homework time. Listening to music may be the best alternative.

Persistent problems

Some difficulties with handwriting are more persistent, especially when they are linked to learning difficulties such as dyslexia. Under these circumstances your child may need particular additional help from you, teachers at her school or a private tutor who has specialised in her difficulties. Sometimes children with dyslexia work better with a word processor. They still have to cope with selecting the correct letters and getting close on spelling, but the keyboard removes the effort of forming the actual letters.

Illustrations in work

Homework will often need to include illustrations of one kind or another. Here are some general rules:

- Make diagrams or maps large enough to show all the relevant details. Do not squeeze writing in around them (except for the title and relevant labelling).
- Every illustration should have a title to explain briefly what is shown. Sometimes it is appropriate to write down the source of the illustration (from what book or article it has been copied).
- Many illustrations need labelling – for instance, names of

GOOD STANDARDS IN HOMEWORK

countries on a map, the two axes on a graph or the parts of scientific equipment. Wherever possible, this writing should run in the usual direction, so that readers do not have to spin the exercise book around in order to read the labels.
- Sometimes your child will need to stick in illustrations of photocopied resource material. These need to be given enough space and, ideally, be close to the relevant part of the written work.
- In an essay or a longer project, illustrations are added for a reason. Your child should usually be writing something about the map or graph, not just drawing it in and leaving it with no comment.

Dealing with errors

Everybody makes mistakes sometimes. Your child may realise that her maths calculation is wrong, a word is mis-spelled or he has missed out a question or a vital point. Generally, she will do some work in rough first and then copy out a final version, but it would be unrealistic to expect him always to do this two-stage system. Also, it is worth bearing in mind that children will not have this choice in tests or exams. It is worth developing a good approach

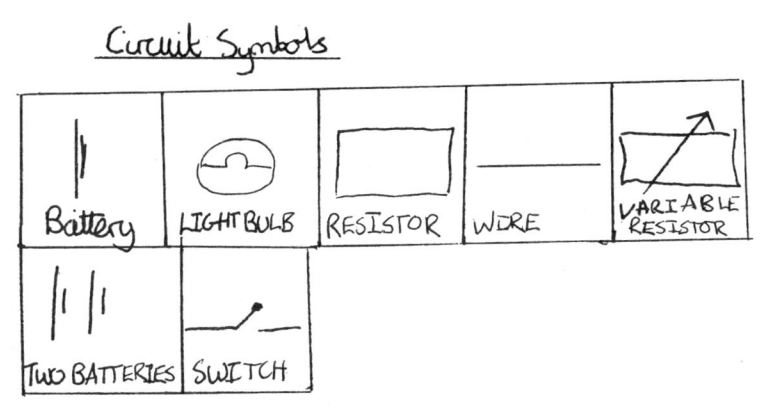

Figure 5 Useful labelling of a diagram

to correcting mistakes on homework and then this can be used when there is no other option. The following are generally acceptable ways of correcting mistakes:

- Remove or cross out the mistake neatly. Either put one or two lines through the botched calculation or wrong sentence – do not make a furious scribbling over the top. Mistakes in pencil can be removed by a rubber and some correcting pens/fluids make a neat job of dealing with ink or biro, although some teachers ban this method.
- Make the correct version obvious. Your child needs to make it crystal clear which is the correct version. A neat line or two will show that one calculation is to be ignored or that the first few lines of an essay have been re-written.
- Make insertions and additions as neatly as possible. Single letters and the odd word can probably be neatly added by making a slash / in the appropriate place and then writing the missing letter or word just above that section. Larger amounts of writing cannot be pushed in with this method and wild drunken arrows do not add to the neatness of a page. Use a method such as placing an asterisk * where the missing text should go and add the missing section at the foot of the page. A note such as "see below" may also direct a teacher's attention.

If your child is having to deal with a great many corrections and insertions, then she may not be taking as much care as she could in planning the homework or in thinking before his pen hits the paper.

Personal touches in presentation

Teachers will tell pupils if there is a particular way that they wish work to be laid out or completed. Scientific experiments, for instance, have to be written up following a specific pattern (see page 65) and diagrams of apparatus have to be accurate and well labelled. However, some homework will leave scope for personal touches such as illustrations or the use of colour in a creative way. Teachers will tell pupils if they are over-doing the creativity.

Effective essay writing

Essays are a necessary form of work in many subjects. The essay may be relatively short, perhaps only a page, but some wili be part of project work that stretches into several pages in total. Most essays will have the same basic structure:

- An introduction that briefly sets the scene for the essay.
- A series of points laid out in several paragraphs.
- A conclusion that reviews the main points or findings. No new material should be brought in at the conclusion.

Planning an essay

A choice of topic

Sometimes children are given a specific title to write on. Work in geography or history for instance, is likely to be focused more on the current topic. On other occasions, for instance in English, children are asked to choose their own focus from a general area. You can help your child by:

- Encouraging her to think up and write down a number of possibilities (half a dozen if possible) before homing in on one.
- Looking at the list with your child. Does she feel more interested to write about some of the possible topics? Has she got more to say on some rather than others? Any other reasons for striking out some of the ideas?
- Getting your child started on planning her essay. If a couple of ideas are equal favourites, she could draft a brief plan for each and decide on that basis.

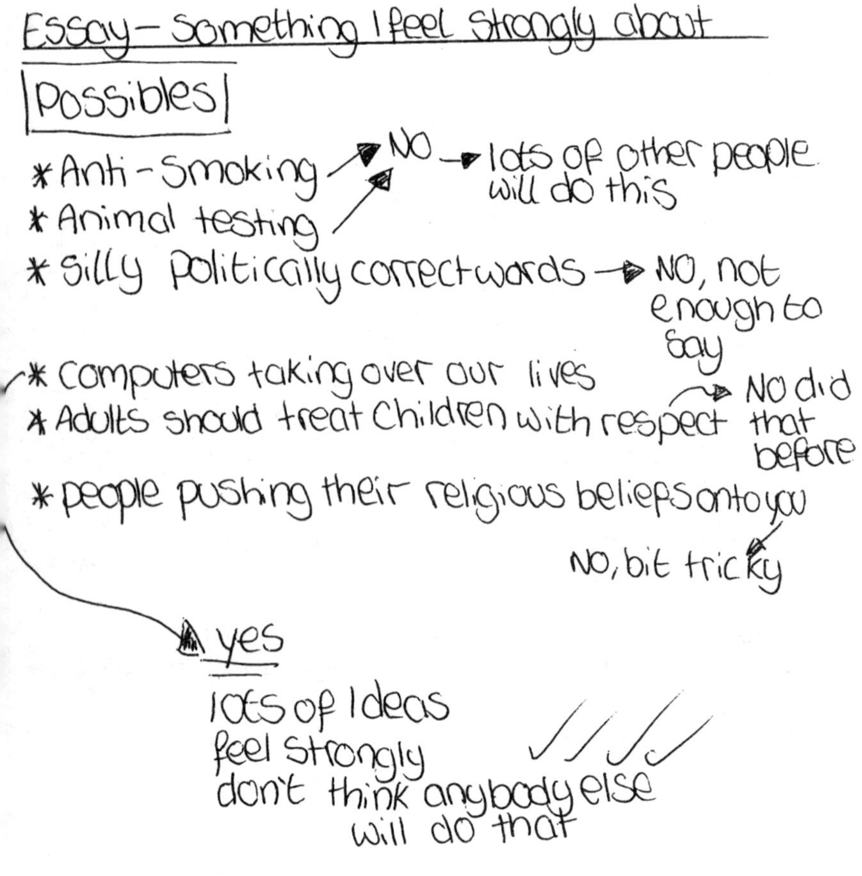

HELP YOUR CHILD WITH HOMEWORK AND EXAMS

Essay — something I feel strongly about

|Possibles|

* Anti-smoking → NO → lots of other people will do this
* Animal testing
* Silly politically correct words → NO, not enough to say
* Computers taking over our lives
* Adults should treat children with respect → No did that before
* People pushing their religious beliefs onto you

No, bit tricky

yes

lots of Ideas
feel strongly ✓✓✓
don't think anybody else will do that

Figure 6 Using notes to think over ideas

Specific topics

It is not usually a good idea to begin writing straight onto a blank sheet of paper without any pre-planning. Some sensible steps to take when writing an essay are given below. Your child can adapt the ideas to suit the different subjects. (The "you" in the tinted boxed points refers to your child.)

What can I write?

- Look carefully at the question or the instructions for homework. What sort of question is this? Underline the key words if this helps.
- Follow the guidance on this essay that the teacher has given. Teachers often give plans or a list of points that should be covered.
- What information do you have already, either in the workbooks or that has been covered earlier in this topic?
- Where might you find more information if you need it, or if it would add a flair of originality to your essay?
- Make a rough plan of your essay. Think of your main points and the minor ones. How will you support or describe your main points? What will your conclusions be?
- A plan might be written in words, with a first, second, third point organisation. Do you find diagrams helpful as a way of planning? (See page 44 for different kinds of diagrams.)
- What is a sensible flow for this essay? Some essays have to follow a logical flow from one point to another. Some descriptive essays, perhaps in history, may follow a chronological flow as well as bringing out the points from the description.
- Do all the points relate to the question? Are the points emphasised in the right way? Have the most important points been given the most space?

With a good plan your child may be able to write an essay straight out. Some children need to work in rough first and then write up a neat, revised version. Sometimes, your child will read her first draft and be able to see that it could be written more effectively in a different order. A few notes can help her to reorganise the material. The better your child becomes at the first plan, the less need there will be to reorganise.

Descriptive essays

Your child will be writing descriptive essays for many of her school subjects. In history and geography, for instance, she will sometimes be writing short answers but on other occasions she will have to write several pages around a theme. Such essays have to cover the facts, but are not one long list of details. There has to be an attempt to weigh up and explain.

Your child might be writing a descriptive essay of what happened in a historical event or coverage of the details of the physical geography of a country. Her teacher will be looking for all the relevant details but also for a clear attempt to:

- Relate events together and follow a sequence of events and the short- and long-term consequences.
- Understand a number of causes and weigh up likely cause and effect when there is no simple answer.
- Be able to grasp the different priorities and values of past centuries and not lay a modern set of beliefs and perspectives over the past.
- Assess the reliability of sources and weigh up the extent to which information can be regarded as unbiased.
- Distinguish between fact and opinion and support any opinions that are expressed.

Analytical essays

In this type of essay your child will be using information to make a point. Analytical essays arise in different subjects, for instance, your child may be asked to analyse an advertisement in a colour magazine, or assess the advantages and disadvantages of different sources of power. The bulleted text below summarises practical points to be considered in an analytical essay. These are relevant, even when your child is writing the shorter pieces of work that will be expected in the early years of secondary school.

A balanced analytical essay

- Give both sides of an argument, so that the essay gives a rounded picture. This should be the pattern even if the essay comes down on one side.
- It is usually best to expand on each point made in the essay and not simply to present points without explaining the importance of how a particular point supports one line of argument. (You would not usually simply list points unless you were asked to give a short answer to a question such as "List the main advantages of . . .")
- Always give your reasons. For instance, "Solar power would be the best alternative here, because . . ." or "This advertisement seems to be playing on parents' worries about their children. I have reached this conclusion because . . ."
- Some essays ask you to take a stand on an issue or to express a clear opinion. As well as the opinion, the essay needs to include your justification for reaching that view or taking a particular stand.

The same kind of preparation and planning can work well if your child is going to present her view in an open classroom debate (see also page 71). You can help your child by listening to the early plans or draft and by offering another point of view – not to argue that it is right, but to help your child support her own view more fully. You might make open-ended comments along the lines of "How would you answer the view that ...?", "You sound as if you are contradicting yourself when you say ..." or "Talk me through why you reject that alternative."

Checking work

Children understandably tend to resist checking work that they have just completed. Their view is often that they have spent ages working on the required pages in the maths workbook, the last thing they want to do now is to check them. It will be counter-productive for you to insist that your child checks every piece of homework. Your aim can be to encourage a habit of looking back through a piece of work in any subject, especially if your child is uncertain about how well she has managed.

If your child will sometimes check back through her work, then this is a good start. Other times she may be prepared to check work with you, perhaps asking you to take a look first. When you are involved in the checking it is important to take a very encouraging line. Make sure that you make complimentary remarks and do not just focus on what is wrong or could be done better. You can point your child to look again without always telling her the mistake. For instance:

- This answer looks very large given the numbers you started with. I'd take another look at the decimal points if I were you.
- You've got three different spellings of "crucial". How about checking which is the right one?

GOOD STANDARDS IN HOMEWORK

- Have you thought about breaking this up with some paragraphs?

Reading through work

However carefully your child has planned and written a piece of work, it is valuable for her to read it through afterwards. This is to check for spelling, punctuation, length of sentence and paragraph breaks. If the work is still in rough then the changes can be made before the neat version is written up. Suitable changes that are spotted in the best version may be managed with some careful erasing and re-writing.

Reading a piece of written work silently will often pick up many points for improvement. However, the most effective method is to read out loud. Your child may be surprised at how much more is picked up when she says her sentences out loud, or you read and she listens. This method often highlights:

- Sentences that are too long or do not have enough punctuation. (Your child, or you, may be desperate for a breath because there are no commas and the sentence has continued for several lines.)
- Sentences or phrases that do not make sense, or which have more than one possible meaning.
- Words or phrases that are used too often in the same paragraph or within the whole piece of work.

Sometimes, of course, it is not possible to check work by reading out loud, for instance, during exams or quiet class work. However, your child's practice in this kind of spoken checking will have helped her to develop a sharp eye for improvements when silent work is required.

HELP YOUR CHILD WITH HOMEWORK AND EXAMS

Reading and making notes

Your child needs to be able to read about a topic and absorb what she has read. As she passes through the school, she will be reading more extensively as well as more difficult resource material. Reading for study is rather different from reading for pleasure. In study, she is reading to extract information that can be used elsewhere. Ideally your child or teenager should not be weighing up every word and phrase but is mentally asking questions such as:

- What are the main points?
- What does this resource tell me that I did not know before?
- What does it confirm for me, from another angle?
- What support is given for the facts or particular perspective?

Making notes

It may be possible to prop up a few reference books at the relevant page and for your child to work the material directly into her homework. She will, however, have to watch out for the trap of copying wholesale. The material must be changed into her own words.

For longer projects and the GCSE coursework, your child will have to read a wide range of material. Unless she converts what she reads into some personal notes, she will not recall the content later. Good notes will also help much later when your child is revising. Revision should not be a time when children and teenagers end up having to re-read all the books.

Here are several practical points about making good notes:

- Notes need to be legible. Even though your child will be looking at her own handwriting, really scrappy notes will be impossible for her to read.
- Always make a clear note of the source of any information – the book or article and the page number. (Your child may

GOOD STANDARDS IN HOMEWORK

want to return for more information and it is very time consuming to search along the lines of "I saw this in one of a dozen books.")

- Sources should be listed at the end of a piece of work. Your child will need to write down the full title of a book or article and the author. It is also worth getting into the habit of writing down publishers and the date of publication of any book, since this information is needed in a proper bibliography for a project or GCSE coursework.
- Everyone needs to try to write notes in their own words. Copying out chunks of a book will not read consistently with your child's personal style. This can be a difficult skill to grasp. Your child could read a section, then look away and say it in her own words, or explain it to you, before writing.
- Sometimes an idea from a book or article will make a good quotation. In these cases, copy out the short extract and note the page in the book where it appeared. The same is true for useful maps or diagrams.
- Useful notes are not simply a shortened version of what is in a reference book. They can be an active attempt to pull out the key points and to relate them to the current piece of work. Your child could underline key points in her notes, using a highlighter pen or different colours.

After all the effort of making notes, your child needs to keep them safe in labelled folders or ring binders with dividers.

HELP YOUR CHILD WITH HOMEWORK AND EXAMS

The use of diagrams

Diagrams, flow charts and different kinds of word maps are a way of organising information on a topic. They can help in the following ways:

- To sort out the main points from the supporting material.
- To give shape to the whole topic.
- To plan a piece of work, so that the main points are clear and have links.
- In understanding and learning a topic.

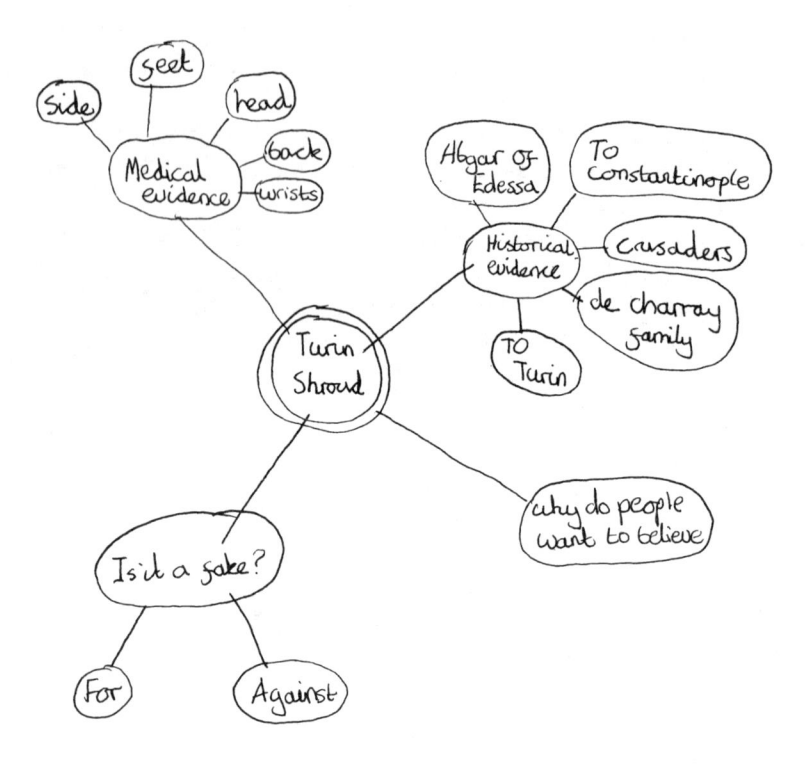

Figure 7 Using a diagram to set out points

GOOD STANDARDS IN HOMEWORK

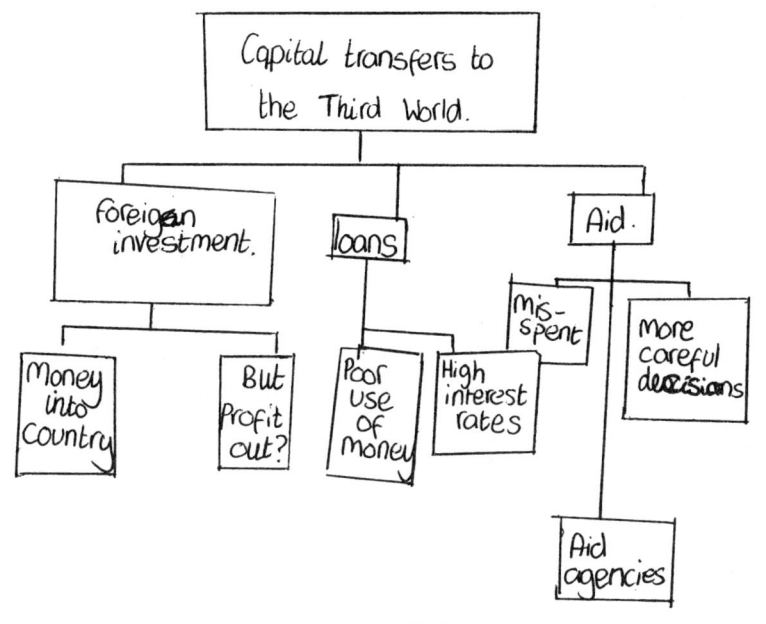

```
                  Capital transfers to
                    the Third World.
                           |
     ┌─────────────────────┼─────────────────────┐
  foreign               loans                   Aid.
 investment.              |                      |
     |              ┌─────┴─────┐         ┌──────┼──────┐
  ┌──┴──┐          Poor        High      Mis-         More
Money   But        use of    interest   spent       careful
into   Profit      money      rates                 decisions
country out?
                                                      |
                                                     Aid
                                                   agencies
```

Figure 8 From main points to related ideas

- In remembering, because the diagram summarises the information.

Your child needs to become accustomed to using material in diagrammatic form, because this will be the best way to present some summary information in a number of her school subjects. It is therefore important that children are not concerned by this approach. It should be her choice how much and in what way she uses diagrams and summary charts to help in the ways listed above. Some children, teenagers, and adults too, find the diagrammatic approach more useful than others.

Diagrams and charts can be made to work most effectively by:

- Keeping the words to a minimum – just key words and phrases to sum up whole ideas.

HELP YOUR CHILD WITH HOMEWORK AND EXAMS

- Using underlining or other highlighting effects to point to major and minor points or different kinds of points in the summary.
- Using colour or highlighter to make parts of the diagram clearer.
- Keeping any lines or arrows very clear as to the links that are being built.

The whole aim is to summarise a complex topic in simple visual form. Diagrams can be helpful, but you do not want your child to spend extraordinary amounts of time redrawing a diagram or flow chart – they are tools to aid study, not artwork for an exhibition.

Your child can steadily improve how she plans and organises her work. It will be useful if she is aware of different ways of approaching her homework but, in the end, she has to decide which methods will suit her best.

It is also important to remember that spelling, punctuation and grammar are important technical issues in writing. It is well worth buying a book for you and your child to consult. I can thoroughly recommend *Better English* by Robyn Gee and Carol Watson (Usborne Books).

CHAPTER THREE

Homework for different subjects

English (or Welsh) as a first language

Your child will be learning the rules for grammar and punctuation but he will also be exploring different ways of using the language in spoken and written communication. He will have plenty of scope for individual ideas but will sometimes have to build these around a given framework. Teachers should provide guidance, perhaps with a written sheet such as the one below.

> *Homework on* Of Mice and Men *by John Steinbeck*
>
> Take the scene in which George shoots Lennie. Write this up as a news item for the Soledad local newspaper. Bear in mind that the news reporter does not know all that you know by reading the book. Any newspaper report has to cover the five Ws: Who? What? Why? Where? and When? Use these questions to plan your report.

Original writing

Children will be given the opportunity to develop their own skills in creative writing in stories, playlets and poems. Your child will have to decide exactly what and how to write but you can offer support if he asks.

Planning and creative writing

- It is generally easier to write around a topic of which you have some experience. Your fiction does not have to be all disguised versions of what has actually happened to you, but it helps to have some link of familiarity to bring events, characters and their feelings alive off the page.
- Good stories are written when the writer has a clear idea about the person or people who are central to the story or play and about the place where the action happens. You need to be able almost to see what is happening through the words that you write.

Stories can have different formats and not all run in a straightforward time sequence. However, your story needs a clear pattern of events:

- You set the scene and then something begins to happen in the story.
- There may be exciting or mysterious parts of the tale.
- Perhaps there is a conflict between the characters or within one character who is torn over what to do.
- The story line is then resolved, perhaps with a twist in the tale. (It is wise to avoid the more cliched twists such as "And then I woke up. It had all been a dream.")

Your own imagination will help you to describe events and draft dialogue.

- Try to imagine how a scene will be experienced by the

HOMEWORK FOR DIFFERENT SUBJECTS

> main character or by "I", if it is written in the first person. Imagine with some or all of the senses – what will it sound, feel and look like . . .?
> - Hold onto the perspective of the person who is central at the moment. If the story is in the first person, told as "I", then all the action has to be told through what this person knows or is experiencing. Stories in the third person may have several characters who move in and out of the action.
> - Aspiring novelists are frequently given the advice to "Show, don't tell". This shifts writing from the blander version of "Gary was very frightened", which simply informs the reader, to "Gary's heart was beating fast. He felt the cold sweat on his face", which takes the reader directly into the character's experience.

Poems involve a different kind of creative writing. Your child will probably be given a particular form of poetry to try, and not all poems are expected to be long or to rhyme. Writing poetry requires a weighing of each word, even more than in story writing, because a relatively small number of words can be carrying a great deal of meaning. Your child may welcome some ideas as he considers different words and a thesaurus can help here. Poems can be better judged if they are read aloud.

Analysis and appreciation of literature

Children and teenagers have to discuss books, poems and plays as well as read them. Teachers will guide them in any piece of work. For instance: "The story of Culhwch and Olwen from the *Mabinogion* has been described as the earliest Arthurian tale in Welsh. How does the Arthur of this story differ from the figure in later legends?"

All children and teenagers have to step beyond the basic

HELP YOUR CHILD WITH HOMEWORK AND EXAMS

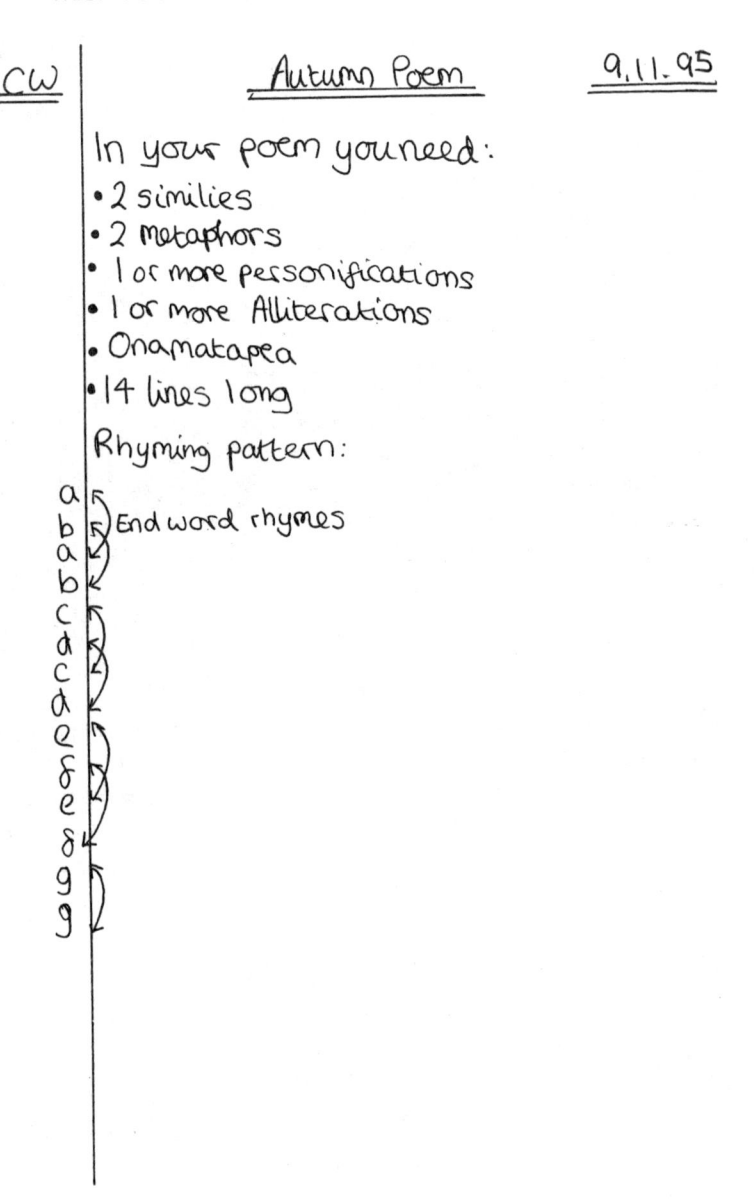

CW | <u>Autumn Poem</u>   <u>9.11.95</u>

In your poem you need:
- 2 similies
- 2 metaphors
- 1 or more personifications
- 1 or more Alliterations
- Onamatapea
- 14 lines long

Rhyming pattern:

a
b ⎫ End word rhymes
a
b
c
d
c
d
e
f
e
f
g
g

Figure 10 A brief from the teacher

HOMEWORK FOR DIFFERENT SUBJECTS

question of "Do I like this book or poem?" and find something to say or write about the piece of work. Some ideas are given in the tinted box.

> **Writing about a play, book or poem**
> - What is the setting in time and place? How is this described? How well do you think it works and why?
> - What is the main plot and any minor themes? How does the plot unfold, how does the author manage surprises, tension or twists in the story?
> - Who are the characters, major and minor? How do you learn about them? What sort of people are they and how do you know this?
> - How does the author use language – the actual words, length of sentence and paragraph? How does the author create an image or bring a scene to life through the words?
> - What is the use of figurative language? Are there examples of similes, alliteration, personification and others?
> - How well does the dialogue work? Does it move the story along or show more about the characters?
> - What kind of message is the author of the poem or other work trying to communicate? Is there any clear moral? Does this work through the story?
> - Can comparisons be made with anything else that the author has written or with similar works written by others?

HELP YOUR CHILD WITH HOMEWORK AND EXAMS

Essay Plan

INTRO:
- Allegorical novel – explain why & how
- Show two varying interpretations
- Reader's view

(Paragraphs min. 4–5 sentences)

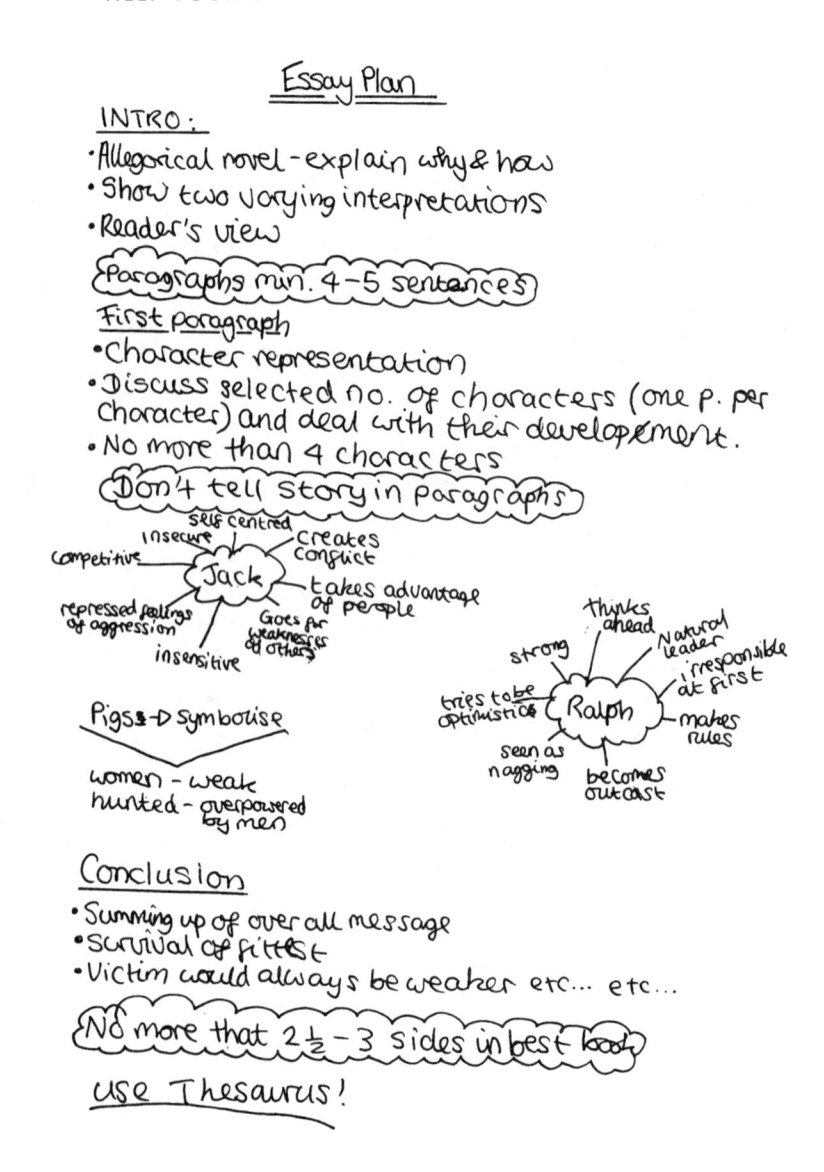

First paragraph
- Character representation
- Discuss selected no. of characters (one p. per character) and deal with their development.
- No more than 4 characters

(Don't tell story in paragraphs)

Jack: self centred, insecure, competitive, creates conflict, takes advantage of people, repressed feelings of aggression, goes for weaknesses of others, insensitive

Ralph: thinks ahead, natural leader, irresponsible at first, strong, tries to be optimistic, makes rules, seen as nagging, becomes outcast

Pigs → symbolise

women – weak
hunted – overpowered by men

Conclusion
- Summing up of over all message
- Survival of fittest
- Victim would always be weaker etc... etc...

(No more that 2½ – 3 sides in best book)

use Thesaurus!

Figure 11 A detailed plan – including the teacher's advice

HOMEWORK FOR DIFFERENT SUBJECTS

Foreign languages

Learning new words

Language teachers give regular tests on new vocabulary, often words grouped around a theme, such as clothes or phrases that a visitor would need in finding the way around a new town.

The focus in language learning is on spoken communication as well as accurate writing, but children still need to come to grips with grammar. This will sometimes mean consigning a list of irregular verbs to memory, in their different forms depending on tense. All the words will be laid out in your child's language workbook, so it does not matter if you would not know the pluperfect tense if it dropped on your foot. You can help by testing your child when she has tried to learn the words (see page 74).

If your own strengths lie in languages then you may be able to help your child or teenager with pronunciation. But, perhaps your memories of French have faded or you never studied any Spanish at all. You can still help because your child's workbook will have the English versions beside the French or Spanish. Your child needs to say the word, even if you cannot correct his pronunciation, because he needs to hear it. He needs to spell it for you to check – either by saying the letters or by writing it down.

English is a language without any accents on the letters, but other European languages have accents as well as nouns that are masculine or feminine and sometime neutral in gender. In spelling out words you and your child can come to an agreement about how he indicates accents. You may use the correct terms, a phrase that you both understand such as "the one that looks like a hat" or you could make a set of cards showing the accents and your child selects one to go with the letter as she spells out the word.

Confusions from grammar

Children learning a second language sometimes have difficulties that can be solved largely by helping them to understand better the

HELP YOUR CHILD WITH HOMEWORK AND EXAMS

mechanics of grammar. Children learn their first language (and a second if they learn it within the family) by speaking. They do not recognise the various parts of the grammar until these are pointed out during lessons on the written version of the language.

If children are vague about grammar, they can be completely lost with an instruction such as "In French the ending of the adjectives depends on the gender of the nouns", or "In German, the verb must go at the end of a subordinate clause". Language teachers do not always recognise this source of children's difficulties. If you think that your child's confusions are being made worse by not understanding parts of speech, then refer to a good grammar book such as the one suggested on page 46.

This problem with grammar is not a new one. I recall being one of a class of eleven-year-olds shouted at by the French teacher who assumed that we were being deliberately awkward. I realised some weeks later, but not with any help from the teacher, that none of us understood the meaning of the words "singular" and "plural". Neither did we understand the useful link for grammar in languages that two or more "I"s make up a "we", a group of "she"s and "he"s make a "they" and, although English does not have a different word for two or more "you"s, some other languages do.

Orals

Part of your child's foreign language work will be to prepare for spoken exchanges. These will take place with his teacher in class and as part of the school exams. An external examiner is more likely to take the oral part of public exams such as the GCSE.

Even in the early months of learning a new language, your child will be practising very simple replies to questions. These exchanges will use the vocabulary that he is learning in the current section of the workbook. As the language work becomes more challenging your child will be expected to reply to questions on a prepared theme, for instance, greeting a friend at a birthday party or arranging to meet at the cinema. You can help your child to

HOMEWORK FOR DIFFERENT SUBJECTS

prepare, even if you do not speak the language well, or even at all. For instance:

- You can ask him the simple questions that he will be facing in the early months of learning. Even if you do not speak this language, your child can help you to make a creditable attempt at the questions. Initially, these questions are of the "What is this?" variety.
- Encourage your child to say his answers clearly and to practise until he feels sure. It is well worth building his confidence in readiness for the harder question-and-answer exchanges which will come later. Children and teenagers can be uneasy about orals if they have not practised well.

During Years 8 and 9 your child is more likely to have to construct his own answers to general questions about where he lives, his family or his hobbies. If your child would appreciate some help then you can:

- Encourage him to think of the kind of answers he could make.
- Remind him to look up any words that he does not know.
- Help him to think of a simpler phrase if his first idea is proving difficult to translate.
- Listen to him practise his replies, in response to your questions.

Absolute honesty is not required in this kind of oral, although it is usually best to keep close to the truth. Creative lying about interesting hobbies may lead to more questions for which your child or teenager is unprepared.

GCSE work in orals involves preparation for simple role plays conducted in the language. Teachers know in advance the range of possible role-play situations and your teenager will be practising his replies.

- If you are not confident in the language, you can still help by giving your teenager the lead in to what he will have to reply. For instance, you might say in English, "The person on the

other end of the phone asks who you are. You reply . . .?" After your teenager's response, you might prompt again with, "Then the other person asks how he will recognise you. And you tell him . . .?"
- Encourage your teenager to say the phrases clearly, to build up his confidence.

In any language it is useful to know how to say "I don't understand" or "Please repeat that", although it would be unwise to overuse these in any language oral.

Maths

Your child will be tackling a wide range of mathematical skills. He should have workbooks or worksheets that take him through the different aspects of Maths. The class work and homework should give him practice so that he can complete the different mathematical operations with confidence.

Maths operates on a system of symbols; it is in many senses a language that can be learned. From the simplest symbols of numbers of 1, 2, 3 etc. to the most complex of formulas, an idea is being communicated through a written symbol. The numbers stand for an actual quantity and symbols like + and × for a particular treatment of numbers. Symbols like = for "equals" are describing a relationship or a next step. A formula is a shorthand for describing a relationship between two or more quantities, forces or other distinct entities.

Helping with Maths

The language of these abstract ideas can cause trouble to children who do not have a flair for maths and who have not been well taught at a younger age. Later work in Maths builds on all the practice that has gone on before. So, children who have become confused will get rapidly out of their depth as they are left more and

HOMEWORK FOR DIFFERENT SUBJECTS

more behind in their understanding. Panic sets in and children can give up on ever managing Maths at all. Children can also have misunderstood or never really grasped the mechanics of calculations and may have developed either very long-winded ways of coping or be following systems that are unreliable for the final answer.

On the other hand, children can be confident in Maths if they have been well taught at school, given enough practice in the different mathematical skills and perhaps helped already by you at home. If your child has a flair for the subject, he will grasp the ideas quickly and wonder why his friends, and adults for that matter, are confused and even unnerved by maths.

Some children with dyslexia, but not all, have problems with Maths as well as with their reading and writing. The difficulties may come with the written instructions for Maths, with understanding and writing the symbols correctly, with problems that involve ordering of symbols or with answers that require an understanding of left and right. If your child is having problems, keep a close eye on how he is managing and if he is really struggling a private tutor may be the best option.

Giving practice

In the early years of secondary school you can help your child with Maths in a number of ways, depending on her level of confidence:

- Give him practice and revision in the basic arithmetical calculations of adding, subtracting, multiplying and dividing. Some children at the beginning of secondary school are still uncertain and making errors.
- Help him to revise her times tables so he knows them thoroughly and the answers emerge almost automatically.

Both of these suggestions will help your child to avoid making mistakes in the basic calculations when he needs to concentrate on learning the new ideas in Maths.

HELP YOUR CHILD WITH HOMEWORK AND EXAMS

Children are encouraged to work with calculators on some problems and are allowed to take their calculator into some exams. Children and teenagers can use the facilities of these handy instruments to avoid the time-consuming calculations by logarithmic tables that you may remember. You can help by encouraging your child to use a calculator confidently but not to depend on it to the extent that he avoids straightforward calculations with pen and paper. Children are encouraged to be adept with calculators but still have to understand what they are doing and be able to show their working.

Talking through problems

It will not usually help if you give your child the answer to a Maths question – assuming that you can work it out quickly. He needs to understand how to reach the answer, so that he can go through the steps next time. You will have to look through the material to work out what to do. So it is far better to take your child with you on this exploration. There are several possible approaches:

- Many workbooks have an example at the beginning of the section. Take your child back to that and see if the pattern helps with the question on which he is stuck.
- Ask your child to explain to you in words what he is doing, as far as he can get. It is hard to help anyone with Maths whilst the confusions are inside their head. Listening to your child will sometimes show up where he has become confused.
- Once your child has a clearer idea of what he should do in a particular kind of question, it often helps to encourage him to speak the steps out loud as he writes them down. For instance, "We want to add two fractions. So, first we have to convert the numbers on the bottom to the same number. If you do something to the bottom of a fraction, you must do exactly the same to the top . . ."
- Sometimes it helps to write out the steps, in words, on cards for your child, so that he can use them with similar problems

HOMEWORK FOR DIFFERENT SUBJECTS

in the future. (Children who are strong in Maths do not have to translate in this way.)
- Sometimes a workbook may give the answers at the back. There are occasions, especially when you are as baffled as your child, when the most helpful way forward is to look up the answer. You may then be able to work the problem backwards and understand the method.
- Be pleased with your child when the light dawns on a particular problem. It may help if you can get him to view Maths problems as a kind of brain teaser and to find the satisfaction of "Gotcha!" when the problem is solved.

Some Maths questions are placed in an everyday context. (The point of a great deal of Maths is that children should understand how to apply it.) However, this requires that children can move in their thinking to and fro between the ordinary situation and the mathematical terms that are used. Again it can help to talk the problem through out loud, emphasising the part of the meaning that is given by the words, the number part and mathematical ideas. For instance, "We want the average speed of the train. That means we have to put total distance on top. That's 250 miles. And total time taken underneath. That's six hours. We divide distance by time to get the average speed. That's 6 into 250 and that gives us 41.67 miles per hour."

Graphs, pie charts or histograms may look different, but they are just a sketch using numbers. You may be able to help your child to approach this kind of Maths step by step:

- Look carefully at the table of figures or graph.
- What does the title tell you? What is it all about?
- Look at the labels on the axes or on the columns and rows. The numbers will relate to that particular topic.
- Follow along part of the table or graph to see what happens. Trace with a finger or hold a ruler along a row.
- Talking through will help again. For instance, "The graph has the number of cars written on the vertical axis and the year on

HELP YOUR CHILD WITH HOMEWORK AND EXAMS

the horizontal. So we can see how many cars were sold in a given year by running a finger up from the right place on the horizontal axis."

Talking through a problem can help your child to generalise to a different question on the same kind of topic. Once your child has a better understanding then he will only need to ask for your help on the odd occasion when he is stuck or if it is a new topic. If your own strengths do not lie with Maths, it is well worth trying to build your child's confidence in the early years of secondary school. Maths will get progressively more difficult and your help may be through more general questions, since the material may thoroughly puzzle you.

Sometimes you and your child will not be able to work out the answer and it is not realistic to hope that you will, every time. The aim then is to get as close as possible.

An example

I was caught with my son's Year 9 Maths with the question of "Mum! How do you get the volume of a hexagonal prism?" The simple answer was that I had no idea.

We took his school workbook and a Key Stage 3 Maths workbook that I had bought and tried to take the question apart. We checked that any hexagonal shape had six sides, looked at a picture of a prism and worked out that a hexagonal prism had to be two normal prisms stuck together. My son then tried working out the volume from other examples in his workbook.

This was one instance when I never found out if he was right in his calculation. I asked a couple of times but the Maths work had moved on. I decided not to press for risk of being seen as a "hexagonal prism bore".

HOMEWORK FOR DIFFERENT SUBJECTS

Maths investigations

Your child will not only be working through the different levels of workbooks, she will also be carrying out explorations known as investigations. In this kind of work children are encouraged to think around a particular Maths problem. There will be some right answers and your child needs to find them. But, he is also expected to:

- Explore and write up how to reach the answer.
- Look for patterns in this kind of problem.
- Write up these patterns in mathematical terms where possible.
- Try some further work on the same topic as an extension of the basic investigation.

<u>Pascal's triangle</u>

<u>Investigation:</u>

```
           1
         1   1
        1  2  1
       1  3  3  1
      1  4  6  4  1
     1  5 10 10  5  1
    1  6 15 20 15  6  1
```

* What is the 8th line?
* Find a pattern for the triangle
* Can you work out a pattern to find the 100th row?

Figure 12 An example of a Maths investigation (Year 8)

Steps in an investigation

Your child's teacher should provide guidelines on how to conduct and write up a Maths investigation. In the early years the account may be more descriptive but he will increasingly be expected to produce a detailed written account.

Maths investigations can seem difficult to children at first. The task needs an open mind and an ability to keep looking at the problem from different angles. What appears to be a fairly simple investigation can take children a long time. So it is not surprising if they are not always very enthusiastic about carrying on with extensions. The most pressing issue is to make a good job of the main investigation. It can help to:

- Break any investigation down into smaller steps and then work through in a methodical fashion. Your child will find the task easier if he takes a logical approach rather than exploring at random.
- Be ready to explain what you are doing at each stage. It may help for your child to make brief notes as he follows up one line of enquiry. It can be hard to recall all the detail when it comes time to write the report.
- Your child has to persevere with different approaches but if he meets a compete dead-end then it is better to note what has happened and take a fresh look at the problem.

Writing up the investigation

The report needs to follow the following order of sections:

- **An introduction** This first section provides a brief description to the investigation. Your child may also be expected to use the introduction like a summary and give a short outline of the work.

HOMEWORK FOR DIFFERENT SUBJECTS

- **Predictions for the investigation** Predictions are much like a hypothesis in science. There needs to be a clear statement of what was expected to be found, but not the actual results – these come later in the report.
- **The results** This covers the work that was done in the investigation. Any relevant tables of figures or diagrams appear here. The report should include all the work that was done on an investigation. Even the lines of enquiry that came to nothing in the end may have shown up something useful.
- **The analysis** Results, whether in words, numbers or tables, need to be explained and not just written in the report and left. If it is important enough to write in the results, it is important enough to discuss and explain. This section gives a discussion of the results:
  - An investigation may have shown consistent patterns or generalisations that can be made to similar situations.
  - This kind of analysis is usually written both in words and in numbers or an algebraic formula, where appropriate.
  - Any formula should be shown to work through written examples.
  - Generalisations need to be checked and any exceptions noted.
  - It is important to explain why a pattern or a generalisation holds for this problem.
  - Any diagrams or graphs need to be explained here.
  - This section of the report is also the place to refer back to the initial predictions and offer some explanation if they have turned out to be wrong.
- **Extension** This is the part of the report where your child tries something extra by working on from the initial problem. Any extension should be discussed in terms of the results.
- **Conclusions** Every report should have a conclusions section, with a brief summary of the main findings. Conclusions are never the place to introduce new work.

HELP YOUR CHILD WITH HOMEWORK AND EXAMS

Science

Science, especially some parts of Physics and Chemistry, also has a language of symbols to stand for events and ideas that may in themselves not be that easy for your child to understand. Some topics will seem easier than others but many have abstract ideas such as energy or forces. The symbols of letters and numbers relate to events that could be understood in everyday language but which can appear strange expressed in symbols and calculations.

If your child has difficulty in relating to this more abstract way of thinking, you may be able to help in much the same ways as have been described for Maths.

The experimental approach

The scientific method is a controlled way of investigating events, and children have to learn its rules. In the early years of secondary school your child will be involved in laboratory activities that encourage him to develop his investigative abilities. He will be writing up some of these for homework.

The essence of early scientific work is that it helps your child to gain experience in:

- Supporting his statements in science with a pattern of "I think ... because ..."
- Planning the work by thinking of possible questions, predicting what will probably happen "If ..." and considering possible ways to make a test.
- Assessing what he knows so far that leads him to these predictions.

The class work in the laboratory should help him to learn the skills he will need to plan and carry out his own investigations:

- What would be an effective method here – a "fair test"?

HOMEWORK FOR DIFFERENT SUBJECTS

- There will be several variables. Which one do you change (the independent variable) and which one do you measure (the dependent variable)? How do you make sure that other variables are not changing at the same time and out of your control?
- What will be the best apparatus and instruments for this investigation and how should they be organised?
- What will be the best way to record the results?
- What do the results mean? Are they what was predicted and if not, why?
- What can be concluded from this investigation?

The report writing of a scientific investigation has some features in common with maths investigations. There need to be separate sections:

- **An introduction** that sets out the aim of the investigation and the predictions.
- **An explanation** of the method used, including a clearly labelled sketch of any equipment.
- **The results** of the investigation, explained in words along with any appropriate tables.
- **A discussion** of the results, what they show, whether they support the predictions.
- **A conclusion** that reviews the findings of this investigation.

Are boys better at Maths and Science?

There has been a persistent belief that girls are going to have trouble with subjects like Maths and the sciences such as Physics and Chemistry. In the past, some exam results have appeared to support this belief but the situation is not that simple.

Some girls do very well in Maths and Science and some boys sink without trace. So it is certainly not the case that "all boys" or "all girls" can be fitted into a neat pattern. Girls seem to do better (as recent exam results show) when an active attempt is made to encourage them in these subjects and counteract any general beliefs that academic success in Maths or Science is unfeminine.

When large numbers of boys and girls are tested on different kinds of mathematical ability, an average difference appears between the two sexes. The girls are, in general, stronger on arithmetical computation, questions that ask for a definition, and applying solutions with which they have had practice. Boys, again on average, tend to be stronger than the girls on problems that require mathematical reasoning and what is called "spatial visualisation" – the capacity to imagine three-dimensional shapes and positions and to think forward to "What will happen if . . ."

These findings are no justification for writing off girls as "No good at maths". The average differences point to the need for some extra and focused help, although not all girls will need it. More boys than girls have difficulties with reading in primary school and are given help in a remedial group, yet nobody claims that boys as a whole are "No good" at subjects that need the written word.

As a parent you need to watch out for the power of expectations and give as much effort to Maths and Science with a daughter who asks for help as with a son. You may have images floating in the back of your brain that still influence you. Illustrations in Maths and Science books now show both males and females, but this was not always the case. For example, in our home we have a substantial reference book on science that dates from the early 1960s. It is still useful, so it sits on the shelf, but our own teenagers noticed that all the scientists in the illustrations are men.

Practical subjects

All children will take different topics within Art; some may have Home Economics and all will take Design Technology. Some of these subjects will have homework but parents are not expected to

HOMEWORK FOR DIFFERENT SUBJECTS

produce the resources of a technology suite, any more than those of the science laboratory. The actual project work will be done with the school facilities and homework will mostly be at the information gathering and design stage. With this in mind your child may be asked to:

- Collect relevant information from local resources, for instance, to research the layout and menus of four local fast food outlets for a project on the design of such restaurants.
- Bring in the ingredients from home for a cooking project. (And you will most likely be expected to pay for materials that your child uses in school, for instance, on his pottery design.)
- Seek out examples for an investigation, for example, into different kinds of packaging or styles of information leaflet.
- Draft a design for an Art or Technology project.
- Write up an investigation in Design Technology.

Design technology

Your child's work in Design Technology may not link in with any of your own school memories, unless you took a specific design course. This subject is taken by all pupils and aims to teach them how to:

- Approach and solve problems of design.
- Express their ideas and reasons in design.
- Make up their designs.
- Evaluate the results of their design in line with the original brief.

Over the school years your child will cover many different topics in Design Technology but his planning and execution of a design will follow similar lines whatever the end product. You will be able to help if you understand the stages that he has to work through as he completes the work and then writes it into a report. The work in the earlier years of school will be less detailed and challenging but will still follow these steps:

Identify the need in detail

- Identify a need for which a design is required. This may be, for example, a plaything that will occupy a fretful baby, or a suitable design for a school bag.
- The statement of the problem outlines what will be the design brief. Effective planning needs a concise statement of what is actually required – for instance, a school bag suitable for secondary school pupils who have to walk to school or use public transport.

Analyse the problem

- The next step is to analyse the problem in terms of more precise information on what is needed to meet the design brief. A number of points would be listed that describe the essential features of the design. Perhaps the school bag must be large enough to carry a normal day's load of books, resistant to rain, comfortable to rest on the shoulders, have several different sized pockets and be available in relatively sober colours.
- Pupils will now carry out some research to gain a fuller understanding of the problem that the design should solve and the possibilities within the design brief.
- Primary research would be the kind of investigation in which children ask other pupils for their opinion or investigate the different styles of bags that are currently used.
- Secondary research would involve discovering what other people have found out, perhaps from books or magazines. Both kinds of investigations can be suitable and the information should be recorded with care, noting the source of any secondary research information.
- Some simple empirical research might be undertaken to investigate some of the features that are planned for the design.

HOMEWORK FOR DIFFERENT SUBJECTS

Develop the ideas

All the work so far on the design has been largely in terms of thinking around the problem and possibilities for the design. The next step is to put some ideas into action:

- Sketch the proposed design, with a clear drawing that shows all the relevant features and label it to explain what is involved. In later years your child may well do several sketches of possible designs and use them to explain how he has reached the decision for a final design. All the sketches have to be clear, but children are not all expected to be talented artists.
- Develop the chosen design in detail, with a further sketch if necessary and make considered decisions, with reasons, about the materials that will be used and the methods of manufacture. As your child's design work becomes more challenging, he will need to consider seriously whether he can make up the design and, if not, to modify the plans.
- Make up the design, test it in the appropriate conditions and write up the whole report.

Helping your child

However good you are at design, it will not help your child if you take over her project and do the sketches or make up the design. You can help by guiding him through the various stages if he is confused or making the mistake of skimping on any of the steps. In the early years of studying Design Technology children may not realise that a design "sketch" nevertheless has to be clear and well labelled; it is not a sketch like a drawing in art.

You may also be able to help by talking about the design brief with your child. Open-ended questions might help him to shape up his thoughts and plans. For instance:

- What is the most important feature of this school bag?
- What do you know from your experience of kites? What do they need to fly with any success?

- What are the possible materials for your baby's plaything? What do you know about babies that might restrict the materials you use?
- What do you think is the advantage of this design for the packaging over that one?

As with any other school work you can also help by showing an interest in the project that your child is doing and perhaps helping him to find some lingering enjoyment in a project that has continued for a long time. You may find yourself helping out in unexpected ways with a technology project. For instance, my daughter's Year 8 project on packaging required hard-boiled eggs. They were to be dropped from different heights to test the effectiveness of the packaging systems that the different groups had developed. Although my own egg had flaws that led it to be eliminated from the final test, I was still delighted that my daughter's group designed the packaging system that protected the famous "three-metre egg".

Preparing to speak in class

Sometimes your child's homework will be to prepare to get up in class and make a short presentation on a topic or argue one side in a debate. This type of activity can arise in different subjects, not just English (or Welsh).

Your child needs to carry out several tasks to prepare for her talk:

- He has to decide what he will say.
- He needs to organise his points in a sensible or logical order – with a strong beginning and end, and a smooth flow of points in between.
- He should make herself notes if this is appropriate.
- He needs to practise delivery and dealing with any nerves about the presentation.

HOMEWORK FOR DIFFERENT SUBJECTS

You can help by:

- Listening to his ideas and talking around the subject as he wishes.
- Asking open-ended questions to help him to think. Never impose your own ideas – it is his homework and he has to make the presentation in the end.
- Trying to follow his flow? Is there an obvious gap in his argument? Do you emerge knowing what are his main points or overall conclusion?
- Checking to see if he knows the content well enough to look up from his notes (if he is using them) at regular intervals.
- Making sure that any visual aids he is using, such as pointing to a map, are large enough for an audience to see.
- Timing the presentation for him so he knows exactly how long it lasts. He may have been given a time limit. It is always better to cut some of the presentation than to try to say it faster.
- Encouraging him to speak clearly and steadily. Presentations are better given slightly slower than most people's conversational pace.
- Being a genuine audience for your child – interested, friendly but serious enough to give him practice with questions, if this will be part of the presentation.

There will be no need to press all these ideas on your child for the first ever speaking out in class. You can share some practical suggestions and help to build his confidence through practice at home. Later, remember to ask him how it went.

Difficulties with a subject

Sometimes your child will be frustrated with one piece of work but otherwise feel confident to cope with the subject. On the other hand, problems may continue to arise with a particular subject.

Buying additional books

It may help to buy a relevant workbook for a particular subject. You will find series on all the school subjects which are linked to the different Key Stages in the National Curriculum. Key Stage 3 covers Years 7, 8 and 9 in secondary school, approximately the eleven- to fourteen-year-olds. Pupils in Years 10 and 11 are working at Key Stage 4 – the fourteen- to sixteen-year-olds.

Make sure that any workbooks are at the correct Key Stage in the curriculum and glance over them first to ensure that the layout looks useful. If you are not getting much help from your child's school workbook, you do not want to buy a similar publication. You will probably want plenty of clear definitions, explanations and worked examples.

An informative workbook to which you can refer will probably be the most useful. Your child is unlikely to be willing to do extra work with question and answer workbooks. He will feel, not unreasonably, that he has enough time taken up with homework.

Talk with the teacher

You should make an appointment with your child's teacher if he continues to struggle. Teachers do not always realise that a pupil is having difficulty and may be able to offer suggestions or more helpful direction in class.

Paying a private tutor

Parents cannot solve all their children's study problems or often cannot prepare them for specific exams. Paying for extra tuition may be the most sensible approach when:

- The stresses of trying to help are affecting the relationship between you and your child.
- Your child has specific learning problems, such as dyslexia and a private tutor is experienced in offering help for this particular difficulty in study.

HOMEWORK FOR DIFFERENT SUBJECTS

- Your child is being left more and more behind in the class work, with no realistic hope of catching up with the level.
- Your child's teacher is not helping with the difficulties and you have reached the limit of what you can do.
- The school really has not assigned enough time in school years or hours per week. Sometimes schools try to squeeze in, say, another foreign language and your child is not getting enough practice or the subject is being taught at a very speedy pace.
- Your child has to sit a specific public exam such as Common Entrance or he is looking seriously ill-prepared for one of his GCSEs.

The best way to find a local private tutor is to ask other parents. Ideally you want to use someone who is known by another family. An alternative is to look for local advertisements by private tutors, but do meet and talk with the person before you decide. Check his or her qualifications and references.

The advantage of a good tutor is that your child will get more focused attention than in a school class. A great deal of personally relevant teaching can be covered in a solid hour of work. The tutor homes in specifically on what your child does not understand and the level at which he is at the moment.

Different helpers

There will be many occasions when you can help your child with the different kinds of homework. You will not feel equally confident in all school subjects but it is important not to give up hope of being of assistance to your child or teenager. You may still be able to help or encourage him to ask someone who does understand the topic. Older brothers and sisters can be a great help, as can friends. By the early teens, boys and girls can find pleasure themselves in sharing knowledge and helping someone else to learn.

CHAPTER FOUR

Preparing for tests and exams

Helping with class tests

You can help your child prepare for tests in the short time before she is due to sit one, but the help that you give her with homework will be equally valuable because you are supporting her to work well throughout the syllabus, rather than focusing on a rush to catch up for a test. You support your child by encouraging her to see the value of paying attention in class and resisting the temptation to drift off a subject because the teacher is disliked or boring.

Your child may have to memorise or revise her understanding of:

- Spellings.
- Times tables (revision in Year 7 of primary school work).
- The new vocabulary of foreign language work or short replies to a range of related questions.
- Detailed information in science.
- The material covered in the recent workbook section in, for instance, geography or history.
- A poem or short extract of a play.

PREPARING FOR TESTS AND EXAMS

- A series of formulas in maths or science.
- Definitions or theorems.

Different ways of memorising

There are a number of possible techniques to help anyone learn material by heart. Different approaches work for different kinds of material. However, individuals also vary and you will need to see what suits your child.

The look-cover-try-check method

Your child needs to put some effort into familiarising herself with the material before she tests herself or asks you to help. She needs to look carefully at the information, not just stare at the page of the workbook. Some children find it most helpful to say the material out loud and others like to write it out. Writing out can help with learning the spelling of vocabulary, since the sheer act of writing is another way to help the pattern of letters enter long-term memory.

Lists of separate items of information can be practised and learned with the look-cover-try-check method. This works well for the meanings of words, spellings or times tables. It also works well for memorising a poem. The steps are given in the tinted box.

> ### *Steps in look-cover-try-check*
>
> 1 Look carefully at the material you have to learn.
> 2 Cover the book, or the side with the answers, and try to say, or write out, the material you have been learning.
> 3 Check how close you are to the correct answer. Or ask someone else to test you.
> 4 Practise again and see how much closer you are.
> 5 Take a break and then try once more.
> 6 See how well you have remembered after the break.
> 7 Focus your practice on the few examples left that are causing you trouble.

Children can follow the sequence on their own but you can be especially helpful to your child since you can hold the book or the work sheet and test your child.

- Listen as she says the poem and prompt gently when she falters.
- Check her times table as she goes along.
- Say the words she has to spell or of which she has to know the meaning, so that she can concentrate on saying them or writing them down.
- Help her check how close she is with her answer. Sometimes it makes sense to give her the correct version as soon she goes wrong. If she is speaking her reply then instant feedback is best. If she is writing down the items, perhaps the spelling, then it is more effective to finish the list and then check them.
- Be very encouraging of what she has got right and any improvements over the last try.
- Look for any tips for how she could remember the items that are hardest for her to recall (see page 77).
- Encourage her to try again, perhaps after a break.

Increasingly your secondary school child will have to commit information to her memory that is long buried in your mind. It does not matter that your mark out of twenty would be seriously embarrassing if you were tested on this information right now. Your child's workbook will be sitting on your lap as you test her learning. The same process applies if she is learning definitions of words and terms and you would not have known where to start. Parents are not expected to know or remember everything; that is why pupils have workbooks with neat tables and lists.

Your child will learn a great deal of information by heart, using the look-cover-check-try method, especially with your encouragement and active help. Practice does make perfect with some material, but some kinds of information will prove hard for your child to learn and recall. Some additional techniques may help.

PREPARING FOR TESTS AND EXAMS

Mnemonics

A mnemonic (pronounced as nem-on-ic) is any kind of memory device to prompt recall. Some mnemonics are nonsense sentences or phrases that use the first letters of each of the objects or ideas that need to be remembered. For instance:

- Every Good Boy Deserves Fun is the common mnemonic for remembering the names of the notes laid out on lines of written sheet music. All Cows Eat Grass is the reminder for the notes that fall between the lines.
- Never Eat Shredded Wheat is a tip for remembering the order of the points of a compass, going in a clockwise direction.
- Richard Of York Gave Battle In Vain lists the colours of the rainbow (red, orange, yellow, green, blue, indigo, violet).

Mnemonics can also be single words made from the initial letters. These are called acronyms. For example, MRS GREN is a shorthand for remembering the seven characteristics of all living things – Movement, Respiration, Sensitivity, Growth, Reproduction, Excretion and Nutrition.

Mnemonics may be rhymes or chants. For instance:

- The spelling rule of "'i' before 'e' except after 'c'."
- The rhythmic saying about days in the months that starts with "Thirty days hath September, April, June and November . . ."
- The chant for spelling "difficulty" that starts with "Mrs D, Mrs I, Mrs FFI . . ."

Some mnemonics are widely used but you can also make up your own family memory joggers. Making up a mnemonic is part of active learning and will help your child to start the process of memorising. The only guideline is that any memory aid should be easy to transform for the person who is doing the memorising. The whole point is lost if your child has trouble remembering the mnemonic.

There would be no point in trying to make up mnemonics for

everything that your child has to commit to memory. The device is useful for material that is proving tricky to memorise. Nonsense phrases, words or short rhymes can help the first stage of learning and then active recall.

Remembering by association of meaning

Sometimes it can help to fix information by association. Once again, any associations of sound, vision or funny links have to make sense to your child. They tend to be very personal associations. For example:

- Perhaps your child is having particular difficulty in remembering some French versions for common English words. Can she make a link that will ease her task? Perhaps "plancher", the French for floor, can be linked with "plank" which is linked with floor rather than ceiling.
- A fourteen-year-old of my acquaintance had difficulty with the French word "celibataire" for single, as opposed to married, until he made the link of "celibate" and the amusing rider that single people are not necessarily celibate.
- A thirteen-year-old I know had difficulty in recalling the letter in the periodic table for potassium, since it is K and this had no obvious link to the chemical. However, she felt that potassium reminded her of the list of vitamins and minerals on breakfast cereal packages. This association took her to "Special K" cereal and the link was fixed.

The examples above are not direct suggestions for what you and your child could do. These particular links may not capture your child's imagination at all and so will not help her. She, perhaps with your help, has to reach her own meaningful associations.

A visual association

People who make a living out of performing feats of memory often use a system of visually linking unrelated items of information by

PREPARING FOR TESTS AND EXAMS

means of a sequence that makes sense to them. For example, they may imagine each item of information written on a different part of their living room or as part of a familiar train journey.

Some people use their visual imagination more than others, so this is probably not a system that suits everyone. However, your child may find it helpful. The steps are given in the tinted box.

> 1 Make a list of all the relevant items of information.
> 2 Walk around your home or bedroom with the list and imagine placing each separate fact onto a different place. (This approach does not work unless you really imagine this clearly.)
> 3 If you want to place items of information along your bus route to school then do this, sitting in one place, with your imagination.
> 4 Then practise, from a stationary position, retrieving the information, item by item, by imagining that you are walking around your home or travelling to school.
> 5 It will be worthwhile practising the retrieval of the information again in the future, since recall may become rusty over time, if there is no practice.

This system may help your child with lists of separate facts but could also work with memorising a poem or section of a play, since one or two lines of the poem are "fixed" to a particular place.

Using diagrams

Summary diagrams can be a useful study aid (see page 44) but they can also help recall of information. The whole point of such maps and diagrams is that they offer links between different groupings of information. Any diagram should have a layout that makes sense to your child, so she should have less trouble visualising the layout in her imagination than a page of a textbook.

Revision for exams

Revision is not just an enormous memorising feat. Recall from memory is, of course, involved but exams are also a means of assessing what your child has understood. Revision can be the last step in bringing a subject together for a child or teenager, so that the different parts of a topic make sense as a whole.

Over the school years your child will develop her own best system of revising but you can help. If you support her to develop a positive approach to revision from Year 7, she will have a suitable range of skills by the time she is facing GCSEs.

How parents can help – some dos and don'ts

Do remind your child that she needs to revise and offer her help.

Don't nag – it is not helpful to say "You've got to get on with it" without offering any constructive suggestions.

Do encourage your child to organise herself to cover all the necessary revision.
Don't insist that she uses only the methods that you find helpful.

Do offer your child help with "Is there anything that I can do?", "Do you want to be tested yet?" or "How's it going?"
Don't insist "You must let me help you" or comment "Shouldn't you have learned that by now?"

Do make sure that your child knows that you are willing to help and, if you are busy right now, when you will be available.
Don't hover over your child or insist on when and how you will help.

PREPARING FOR TESTS AND EXAMS

> **Do** acknowledge that your child is working hard and that you are confident that she will do her best.
> **Don't** undermine her hard work with vague jolly remarks such as "Cheer up" or "It's not the end of the world". Certainly no child or teenager wants to be told "Your brother never had this kind of trouble with revision".

Getting organised for revision

You have to revise

You may need to explain to your Year 7 child that revision will be necessary; some children do not realise. Teachers should be helping the children as well, by alerting them to the importance of revision, discussing how effective revision can be done and giving summary sheets of the topics covered.

A revision timetable

A revision timetable does not need to be very complex. A simple breakdown of the available time is likely to work better than trying to allocate every hour and half hour. You certainly want to dissuade your child if she is spending a great deal of time redrafting and beautifying her revision timetable, rather than getting down to the actual revision.

Here are some practical points about revision:

- Your child's timetable should probably start two to three weeks before the beginning of any internal school exams. There is not much point in starting revision earlier than this point. (A longer period of revision will be necessary for more demanding exams such as the GCSEs.)
- It is worth trying to complete a topic within one revision session but there is no need to attempt to complete entire subjects before moving onto the next.

Revision Timetable

Monday: History and French
Tuesday: Geography and Maths
Wednesday: English and Science
Thursday: Design Technology and History
Friday: Information Technology and Geography
Weekend: French, Maths and Religious studies
 * Get Dad to test me
 * Ask Mum about the Technology project

Monday:

Figure 13 A simple revision timetable

- The serious risk of working without a timetable is that the revision will be unevenly spread over the subjects. Perhaps your child will be so concerned about science that she leaves her French to very late on and is then in a panic about all the vocabulary that she appears to have forgotten.
- It is unwise to assign a lot less time to a subject because your child feels it is her easy subject. She should at least give some time to looking through the year's material so that he can confirm, or not, that the subject is firmly in his mind.

PREPARING FOR TESTS AND EXAMS

- As your child works through the first week of her revision timetable she will gain a fairly accurate view of how fresh her memory is of the different topics and how much work may be needed to be ready for the exams. She may find it useful to note down the various topics in each subject that have to be covered.

Revision of the different subjects

Your child may not need identical amounts of time on the revision timetable for every subject, nor will the kind of revision she is doing be the same. For instance:

- Her work in French may be mainly refreshing his memory of all the vocabulary that has been covered in the year, irregular verbs and useful phrases. She may welcome your help with testing when she is ready.
- Her revision for Maths may be looking carefully through the work of the school year and practising those methods which she knows she finds more difficult. There may also be formulas and theorems to commit to memory.
- Geography and History may have a wide range of information that your child needs to refresh and know well enough to be able to produce for exam questions.
- Science may be a blend of general information on the three sciences. The subjects will also include definitions, some formulas or lists of related information that have to be memorised.

Some subjects may have a practical exam for which your child has to prepare, but the work will be done in class on a given day. For example, the Design Technology revision may be to plan the design of a piece of luggage for weekend trips. Your child would then be thinking about the factors to consider, gathering all the necessary information and making preliminary sketches. She would take all her notes into the exam and produce a neat and full version of the design within the time limits.

HELP YOUR CHILD WITH HOMEWORK AND EXAMS

Taking breaks

It will not help if your child tries to do several hours of uninterrupted revision study. She will lose freshness after twenty to thirty minutes, her mind will wander and she will not recall much of what she has been looking over. Children and teenagers find their own best way of breaking up the work. A possibility is to take short breaks every twenty to thirty minutes of study. The break should definitely include looking up from the books, perhaps getting a drink and walking about the home. Your child will not be doing much more useful work after a couple of hours of study and will need to take a longer break.

Breaks are necessary for effective revision and only become a disruption if children are distracted from returning to their work. Parents can help by a gentle reminder to get back to the revision. You can also help by not being the distraction yourself by requiring your child to help with some domestic chore which could wait.

Organising the material

Without doubt, good notes from the year's work will support your child in her revision. Previous hard work will now pay off. The tough work of revision in the first year of secondary school may be the way that your child learns that it is worth doing homework and class work well in the first instance.

It is worth completing any work that was unfinished. However, pupils who have to make up a great deal of work at the same time as revising will be severely overloaded. Secondary schools take the reasonable view that it is pupils' responsibility to make up any work missed through illness or from family holidays taken in term time. (Schools do not like families taking children out of school for holidays because of the disruption to children's work.)

Revision time may also be the way that your child finally understands that good presentation of work is not just for his teachers. It can be a sobering experience for children to look at pages of vital work in a subject that they can hardly decipher because they took

PREPARING FOR TESTS AND EXAMS

very little care at the time. Children may have to gather all their notes and books together and smooth out crumpled pieces of paper – it depends on how neatly your child keeps her work. It is worth placing any loose notes together in the same file or folder.

Summary notes

In the early years of secondary school your child may not need to make summaries, if the material is very clearly laid out in his exercise and workbooks. In later years, the subjects may cover a great deal of material and the revision can be made more manageable by making summary lists or diagrams of key points. These might be the key factors in coastal erosion or the enzymes involved in digestion, for example.

The advantage of making brief notes, on a separate sheet or cards, is that this will help your child to look over the material in an active way, rather than skimming without really registering. The whole point is that these are very short summaries, not lengthy re-writes of the material. Your child can organise her lists or diagrams in a logical way for the material and use headings or highlighter pens to make the points clear.

Your child will need to learn some definitions, for instance in science, by heart but it will not work for her to learn entire essays by heart or to fix very exact essay plans in her head. She is very unlikely to be given the same question in the exam and needs to have the information easily accessible in her mind.

Being tested on the material

Part of the revision process for your child is for her to check that she can recall the material. You can help with this checking as well as encouraging brothers and sisters to help test each other. There are different ways of helping:

- Material with clear right or wrong answers can be checked by asking your child the relevant questions. These may be a list of

words or phrases in vocabulary, definitions in Science, or formulas in Maths or Science. She may say or write the answer, and you should both check whether it is correct and practise again, perhaps after a break (see page 75).
- Subjects like Geography or History have a broad sweep of information. You can help your child test her knowledge and understanding by asking more general questions, such as "Tell me about the economic development of Japan" or "Talk me through the events of the Crusades".
- With several pages of relevant information, you then have to keep your eye on the book – your child's exercise or work book – and pick up on what she is missing out. You can help with prompts such as "And what was the date of that?" or "You've missed something out. It's something to do with Japan and fossil fuels . . ."

SATs in Year 9

SATs assess the usual syllabus

It is possible for either teenagers or their parents, or both, to get very concerned about SATs (Standard Assessment Tasks). Undoubtedly, they are an important national testing programme. However, so long as your teenager has established a good pattern of revising towards exams, then it is questionable whether he should be working in a different or more extensive way for the SATs. If your teenager has failed so far to take exams with sufficient seriousness, then Year 9 and the SATs may be an important opportunity for parents, and hopefully teachers, to be very persuasive about the consequences of not bothering.

The tests are an assessment on the syllabus that your teenager's teachers should have been covering with the pupils throughout the year. SATs do not suddenly introduce new material, so there is no necessity for parents to rush out and buy additional books. The teachers should be covering the syllabus and giving pupils practice in the different kinds of questions that they will encounter once

PREPARING FOR TESTS AND EXAMS

they sit down to complete their SATs. Pupils will not be entered for extension papers in any subject unless their teachers judge that they are really capable. Any Year 9 pupils entered for these additional papers should already be tackling a level of work that is usually not covered until Year 10 or 11.

Additional workbooks?

If you think that your teenager might benefit from extra practice, then you will find useful workbooks on the SATs for different ages in the education section of any good bookshop. It would be wise to talk with your teenager first, rather than simply present her with any workbooks and tell her to complete them. Ask your teenager if she thinks any extra work might be useful and go together to choose any workbook. Alternatively, you can go with a shopping list of her choosing. Perhaps she will say "I wouldn't object to a bit more practice on Maths" or "You can get me a Science booklet, but make sure it's got plenty of Chemistry in it."

Exam technique and SATs

There have already been examiners' reports on previous SATs, which include general comments about common and avoidable mistakes and how pupils overall have coped. These reports have highlighted some very practical suggestions, but none are specific to sitting the SATs. The national tests are simply another set of exams for your teenager and the practical advice in Chapter 5 will be relevant.

Preparing for exam conditions

Realistically, your child's school has to organise the full-scale exam conditions practice. They will achieve this by having children and teenagers sit "mock" exams, for instance for the GCSEs. Teachers should arrange this kind of practice for children

HELP YOUR CHILD WITH HOMEWORK AND EXAMS

who are going to sit any important external exam or audition.

You cannot create exam room conditions in your own home. However, you can obtain previous exam papers for your children and teenagers if the school is not arranging this practical step or your child would like to practise at home. (See page 134 for obtaining GCSE exam papers.)

Selective entrance exams

Some state schools and the City Technology Colleges (CTCs) have a selection process to determine prospective pupils' level of ability or aptitude in particular subjects. Selective assessment should never be a secret process. The school brochure should explain clearly about any exam, interview, and so on.

Common entrance for independent schools includes exams that cover the whole National Curriculum. Past papers can be obtained from Common Entrance Publications Ltd, Jordan House, Christchurch Road, New Milton, Hants BH25 6QJ. Tel: 01425 610016. You would have to contact direct any independent school that has its own entrance exam.

Preparing for orals

Your child will have an oral exam as part of the foreign language assessment. Spoken as well as written use of language will have been part of her curriculum from the beginning. There are ideas on page 54 as to how parents can help.

Sometimes, a face-to-face interview is part of the assessment process in an examined course. An examiner is usually discussing a candidate's coursework projects. This kind of oral is less likely in your child's GCSE programme but becomes increasingly more common with more advanced courses.

PREPARING FOR TESTS AND EXAMS

Preparing for an oral on your work

The best preparation for this type of exam is to:

- Look afresh at your coursework – the ideas and arguments, the methods and findings in a piece of research, any problems and so on. Be clear about your main points so you can express them clearly.
- Be ready to explain anything in your work that is unusual or likely to be challenged. Support your comments with reasons and offer alternative explanations, if that is appropriate. If you know there are weak points in your work, then be prepared with the most sensible explanation you can offer.
- Prepare some balanced answers to the kind of questions that you may get asked and practise saying them, perhaps to your parents or a friend. You may not be able to predict the questions exactly, but themes are likely to centre around "Why?", "What?" and "How?". Do not rehearse exact answers word for word but have some clear themes that you can follow.
- Be sure that you can say something sensible and positive to "Why did you choose to look at . . .?", "What made you select the method of . . ." or "How did you decide on . . .?" Answers should be positive and be ready with a reasonable explanation for any mistakes that have become obvious with hindsight.
- Try to give more than one- or two-word answers. For instance, questions such as "What do you feel was your most interesting finding?" or "What do you think was the central factor in . . .?" deserve more than "The erosion" or "Local politics". Give at least a sentence in reply.
- Express yourself positively, especially on any aspect of your work that could be criticised. For instance, "Why did you only interview five people . . .?" needs a positive

HELP YOUR CHILD WITH HOMEWORK AND EXAMS

> answer. Replies such as "That's all I could get" or "I ran out of time" are weak. Similar phrases to avoid are "There didn't seem to be any point" or " I don't know".
> - Be ready with a format of reply to deal with questions to which your reaction is a genuine "don't know". Depending on the type of question, your reply might be built around "That's a very interesting way of looking at the problem", "As far as I explored the topic . . ." or "I would like to explore that point in the future . . .".
> - Use any technical terms that are appropriate to your work, but make sure you know what they mean.
> - If you do not understand a question, then ask the examiner for clarification with a phrase like "I don't understand what you are asking . . ." or "I'm not sure, are you asking about . . .?"

Life during revision periods

You can encourage your child to plan ahead with her revision and be available for specific support when she asks. Otherwise any activity on your behalf has to be help in actually getting on with the work. Parents need to show consideration, just as was necessary with the study of homework:

- Tell your child in advance of any family events that could influence his revision schedule.
- Avoid any unnecessary disruptions when your child is working well.
- Do not ban her social life during revision periods but help her to organise it sensibly. Think ahead so that your child's plan to go out with friends, cleared by you two weeks ago, is not suddenly cancelled because "You should be revising . . ."
- Your child may need to plan her social life a bit more, especially if her preference is for spontaneous get togethers.

- Your help may be welcome, to fend off friends on the telephone or at the door – so long as you are not embarrassing. Your daughter may agree that you can say over the telephone, "I'm sorry. Kate is busy right now with revision. Can I take a message?" If pressed, you might be mandated to say, "It's more than my life is worth. She says nobody is to disturb her." This kind of comment is very different from telling your child's friend, " She can't come out. I've told her she's got to revise."

Finishing revision

There is little point in revising right up to the bitter end. Some children or teenagers stand outside the exam room, still looking through their notes, but nothing useful will enter their brains.

It is definitely unwise to be up late the night before, desperately trying to push in more information. Some children find it useful to glance through their summary notes the day or early evening before an exam, but this should be the limit. Some children prefer to stop during the day or even do not revise beyond the first day of the first exam, especially with school exams which are grouped relatively closely together. The GCSE programme, in contrast, stretches over a matter of weeks and some revision in between the exams can be useful.

Learning to revise

However helpful you have been to your child or teenager, she is on her own once she goes into the examination. If you have left your help until the GCSEs you may be very uncertain about whether your teenager is well prepared. The advantage of being ready to help your child from the very beginning of secondary school is that you, and she, have time to learn how to revise, good exam technique (see Chapter 5) and to learn from any mistakes.

CHAPTER FIVE

Sitting exams

Worries about exams

In the weeks running up to exams, a sensible revision plan for your child to follow is the best antidote to rising panic. Exam week itself is not the time for late night television viewing or a highly active social life. However, children do not usually benefit from enforced earlier bedtimes. They tend to lie in bed worrying about the exam or the fact that they cannot get to sleep.

It is not unusual for concerns about exams, like any other worry, to enter children's dreams. You can help by letting your child talk about the dream if he wishes, but stress that this is just one way that anybody's mind deals with concerns. The content of this kind of dream is often so extreme that your child will not see them as likely predictions. Children and teenagers do not normally end up in the Science exam dressed in their night clothes or only have a pen with invisible ink for writing the English exam.

Positive stress

Children and teenagers need to take exams with seriousness and so an overly relaxed approach is not suitable. They should not feel exactly the same as if they were about to sit down and watch a good video. Children need to feel poised to do their best. You can help by explaining that mild stress, such as an empty feeling in the stomach or increased perspiration, is not necessarily a bad sign. On the contrary it is a message that your body is developing that extra edge.

Stress and continuing health conditions

The situation is slightly different if your child tends to develop other physical symptoms under stress. Perhaps your son's asthma can become worse or your daughter's eczema becomes more troublesome than normal. You may then need to be prepared so that your child has to hand whatever medication usually helps. Children with hayfever often find that summer exams coincide with their worst time for the allergy. Fortunately, this generation of children have choices of medication that deal with the allergy without making them very sleepy.

Effective exam techniques

This part of the book is laid out slightly differently from the rest of the book because my aim was that it should be easy to share directly with your child or teenager. The "you" in the bulleted points means the person who will sit the exams – your daughter or son. Please use the section in whatever way is likely to work best for your child. You may want to talk a little at a time about exam techniques, using the pages to clarify your own thoughts and memories about exams. Alternatively, some teenagers might prefer to look at the pages with their parents, or to read through the points themselves.

Take the right equipment

Your child or teenager needs to know the exam timetable and to go into each exam with the correct equipment. This will always include a set of pens and pencils and a ruler but he will sometimes also need a calculator or a mathematical set.

Coping with exam room nerves

Not all children or teenagers feel awful as they face the exam paper. Some feel ready and their approach is one of "Right, here I go". However, if your child is one of those who tends to panic or go blank, then you could help him to prepare for that moment. Here are several options that can help:

- Think positive thoughts and even mutter them – but well under your breath. You might find it useful to tell yourself, "I'll do my best", "I'll just see what they ask" or "I'll take it one question at a time".
- You may find that a couple of deep, careful breaths will help. Then open the paper and get started.
- Or you may find that telling yourself some practical reminders will direct you positively. For instance, you might tell yourself to "Read the questions first".
- You could spend a few moments lining up your watch on the desk or placing your pencils.
- None of these techniques should last for ages. The point is to calm yourself so that you get started.

> *A note to parents*
>
> This generation of parents will be the last one to think just in terms of exam room nerves. Teenagers in the GCSE programme have to organise themselves for coursework which is part of the overall assessment. "Project panic" can overtake a poorly organised teenager with potentially serious consequences on her final grades (see Chapter 6).

SITTING EXAMS

Read the exam paper properly

Children should not be facing exam papers that look completely alien to them. Teachers should have given them experience of the kind of questions and the layout of questions that will arise within an exam. Whatever the layout of the exam, the following practical points will be important:

- Look carefully through all the paper first so that you know the scope of what you have to cover.
- Read the main instructions carefully and re-read them if you are unsure.
- You must be completely clear about how many questions you have to answer. Look closely, sometimes an exam paper may have a series of instructions like "Answer either question 1 or 2".
- Watch out for when the questions begin and end. A question in Geography, for instance, may have some data or a map and then a series of parts to the same question which stretch over several pages.
- Perhaps you have to answer a certain number of questions from different sections of the paper.
- Be clear about what choices you have and then make them.
- Note that some sections of an exam paper will have to be answered by every candidate.
- If the instruction says "Place an 'x' in a box" then do that. If you are asked to tick "two boxes", then do not tick one or three.

Read the questions properly

Examiners' reports for the GCSE and for the SATs regularly state that some candidates appear not to have read the questions with enough care. Children or teenagers throw away potential marks by missing out a part of a question. Every year, in every exam some children answer questions that were not actually asked.

Answer the question

Exams are not an opportunity to empty the contents of your brain in a random fashion:

- Candidates' answers have to relate to the specific question – what it has asked and how you are required to reply.
- Avoid basic mistakes by reading the question carefully. There will be no marks for an essay on the ancient Romans, however excellent, if the question asked about the ancient Greeks.
- Some questions in exams have to be interpreted to an extent and that is part of the answer. But they cannot be twisted dramatically to a topic that you would rather answer.
- Read any key terms in the questions and make sure that your reply deals with these.
- Some questions will have several parts to them. Make sure that you answer each part, as they will all have marks.
- If a question, for instance in Maths, tells you to "Show your working" then do this. You will lose marks, even if the answer is correct, if you fail to lay out how you reached it.

What does the question mean?

At first sight exam questions can seem obscure, and some may be more confusing than others.

- Examiners are not being deliberately awkward. They have to phrase questions that point you toward a topic in the examined subject, without starting to answer the question for you. This will be especially true of questions that require an essay-type answer.
- Somewhere in the coursework you have covered will be the material you need to answer the question. Your job is to spot the link, if it is not immediately obvious.
- Underline or note down key words in the questions to guide you towards what is being asked. For instance, if you are

SITTING EXAMS

asked about the "causes" of pollution in cities, then you need to address points such as fumes from road traffic rather than to list the effects of the pollution such as trees dying.
- Sometimes, of course, you cannot access the information or the wording of the question still seems so obscure that you will be better to select another, when you have that choice.
- If you have to answer a question that is uncertain, then look for key words. What is the question likely to mean? What kind of approach is it probably asking of you?

Read any extract carefully

In some exams, part of a question will include an extract:

- Read this passage – the report, poem or extract from a book – through once carefully and then once again.
- Read the questions that are asked about the passage very carefully. They will direct you to the kind of answer that is wanted and to the kind of analysis you must make of the extract.
- Answer all the questions about the extract.

Different kinds of questions

Different terms

You need to register clearly in what way you are asked to answer each question. It is important to understand the different terms, since giving too long an answer wastes precious time and giving too short a reply will lose you possible marks. You will not encounter all these terms in the Year 7 exams. I have made a full list so you can return to this section several times.

"List..."

These questions mean you to write down all "the uses of..." or "all the reasons why...". It will be clearer to list them vertically down the exam page, with a new line for each item (and not horizontally in one long sentence across the page). A "list ..." question may also direct you with the instruction of "list briefly" or "list as fully as possible". Follow this instruction. Another part of the question may then ask for more information.

"Define ..."

These questions want you to express in words the exact meaning of the given word or phrase, the scientific principle or mathematical theorem. In many cases, you should have learned an exact wording from your subject workbook to produce. If you have to draft your own definition, then weigh your words carefully to convey the exact and full meaning. Definitions cannot include a repetition of the word or phrase itself that is being defined.

"Compare ..."

This kind of question is used to test your understanding of two or more similar items or topics. If you are asked to "compare energy input with energy output" then you are most likely drawing a direct comparison between these two values, probably in a given example. You are not explaining why input is in general different to output as an idea.

"Compare and contrast ..."

This type of question is giving you the chance to describe similarities and differences. Perhaps the question will be "compare and contrast the foreign policies of ..." You need to show knowledge and understanding of both the policies but not write about the two topics completely separately. You might be considering what they have in common, what are the differences, what might appear to be contrasts but are not.

SITTING EXAMS

"Discuss..."

When you are asked to discuss an issue, you are being given the chance to cover all the relevant information, in an organised way. A well planned answer, more likely in an essay format, will communicate facts but also some reasoned arguments, any principles involved, the basis of differences that are covered and so on.

"Describe..."

Questions that ask you to describe mean that you should clearly give the details of the event, equipment or procedure. In mathematical or scientific questions you might be asked to "describe" what you would do to solve a particular problem. You need to lay out the steps in words, but you are not being asked for an explanation of why this procedure works.

"Explain..."

This word is often used with describe as in "describe and explain ..." Although the question may not specifically include a "Why", "How" or "What", you need to plan an answer that covers these kinds of questions as appropriate to the topic.

"Illustrate..."

This word can be another way of saying describe and explain, for instance, "Illustrate your answer with examples ..." You have to make sense of the question in context, because it does not always literally mean "draw" an illustration. Sometimes a map or sketch will be appropriate, but at other time the illustration will be in words. Any graphs or diagrams should always be given a title and appropriate labels.

"Interpret..."

This type of question is most likely to be linked with graphs or tables, that are provided as part of the exam question. The data will possibly be new to you. You have to look carefully at the pie chart or other figure and then describe accurately in words what information the figure provides. What does it tell you? Are there several possible interpretations of the information provided?

"Survey the various factors involved in . . ."

This type of question is asking you to work through the different factors on the given topic. You should not simply list them in brief, but should go into more detail about the nature of the factors to consider, and how they might influence a decision or end result.

"Estimate . . ."

This word is most likely to appear in mathematical questions. You are being asked to make a good guess on the basis of the information that is provided. You are not being asked to work out the exact answer but there will be enough detail for you to get close. For instance, you might be given a circle that has been divided up into parts, and you are asked to judge the size of each portion.

"Evaluate . . ."

Children and teenagers often confuse this term with "estimate". Evaluation is not about making a good guess or a judgement by sight (see above). The question is asking for a weighing up of an issue or a procedure. You might be working through the advantages and disadvantages or assessing the likelihood that a procedure would work or be appropriate.

Multiple choice questions in exams

Some parts of an exam may be presented as a question followed by three or four options. Candidates have to mark the correct option.

SITTING EXAMS

- Look at the instructions on how you are supposed to mark your answer. Is it a tick, a circling or filling in an empty small box? Follow what is asked.
- Unlike the essay-type exam, there is no point in looking for your most favoured questions. The best approach is to start from the beginning and work your way through.
- Read the questions carefully, a missed "not" could utterly change the meaning.
- Complete those questions on which you are sure. Don't spend too much time agonising over ones about which you are uncertain. You can come back to them if you have time.
- If you have time to spare, then go back through and look again at the questions that you could not answer. Choose the option that seems most likely to be right. You may be able to eliminate one or two possible answers as definitely wrong. A blank will get you no marks and your best guess may be correct. It is very unlikely that you will sit exams in which wrong answers will lose you marks. (Check with your teacher.)

Short answers

Some exams will have questions that require more than a tick in a box but do not ask candidates to write pages of an essay. The structure of this type of question varies and this is one reason why teenagers need experience of past exam papers. Some likely possibilities include:

- Questions that ask for a definition of a technical term in the subject. In this instance, answers need to be concise, yet accurate.
- Short answers will be required to questions such as "Give two reasons why ..." or "Name three common uses of ..." These answers need to be clear and full, but should not be a mini-essay. The number of lines provided on the exam paper will be a good indication of the length of answer expected.
- Sometimes a question is started through some information – a

table of statistics, a drawn piece of scientific equipment, a map or an extract from a book. A series of questions are then asked about this information and perhaps also related topics. Answers need to be linked back to the initial information.

Essay questions

Some exam papers will have questions that require an essay as the answer. It is worth choosing the questions with some care, and where there is a choice:

- Choose which questions you think you can answer the best.
- Decide the order in which you will write your essay answers. You may like to start with a question that you feel confident about, so that you get into the flow quickly.
- Bear in mind all the practical advice given earlier on in the section about the likely meaning of terms in any question.

Plan your answers

Even with the sense of pressure in exams it is worth giving a short amount of time to a rough plan for your answer.

- Make a short list of points to direct your writing.
- Put a line through your plan when you have finished so that it is clear this is not part of your answer.
- Do not spend ages fine-tuning your plan. The point of exams is to get down to work promptly – although not so promptly that you make a foolish mistake about what you are supposed to do.
- You will work in a speedy fashion if you have a clear plan of what you are going to do.
- If you are answering questions about an extract, for instance a poem or a town development plan, then make a few brief notes to help you plan your answer. It will be possible to underline parts of the passage on the exam paper. Any discussion of an extract needs to refer to key points in the provided

SITTING EXAMS

written material but should not depend on lengthy quotations. Answers should be in your own words, not chunks from the extract.
- A brief plan will help you to highlight the main points in your answer and to present them in a logical fashion. It makes it less likely that you will suddenly notice a new point when you have almost finished your essay.

Writing good answers

The point about exams is that you are demonstrating what you know. Of course, you have to answer the questions that are asked and not those you desperately wish they had asked, but, within those boundaries, show off your knowledge appropriately.

Giving relevant information

It is important that you take the opportunity to show an examiner what you know, whether you are giving an essay-type answer or short-sentence replies.

- Do not lose marks by being vague in your answers. For instance, perhaps you are asked to list the factors that can affect the birth weight of a newborn baby. A reply of "smoking and drinking" will not do your knowledge credit. The point is that it is the mother's smoking and the drinking of alcohol that are important, plus any other factors you list.
- Undue padding does not usually work in essays but make sure that you do include all the relevant information.
- In literature exams you will be expected to refer in detail to the poem, play or novel. Sometimes this will be a general reference to incidents but you will be expected to use some quotations from the set texts. You are not expected to memorise enormous amounts and, anyway, quotations should not usu-

HELP YOUR CHILD WITH HOMEWORK AND EXAMS

ally be very long. On the other hand, single word quotations will rarely be appropriate.
- Support what you say in an essay and avoid unjustified assertions. Show that you can appreciate both sides of an issue, even where the question is inviting you to come down on one side.

It is unwise for anyone to take undue risks in exams. Higher grades are gained from showing extra knowledge or an original approach, but not for the wilder flights of imagination. For instance, it is better to write well and accurately in your foreign language, using words and grammar that you understand, than to attempt an essay topic for which you do not have the vocabulary.

Using appropriate technical terms

With many subjects it will be appropriate to use the relevant technical words. They will help to provide the best explanation or description.

- Take the opportunity to use appropriate technical language and terms. Of course, you should use any terms in the right context and spell them correctly.
- An analysis of a poem or section of a play can be an ideal opportunity to show your understanding of the different kinds of figurative language. Use terms such as "hyperbole" or "paradox", with appropriate examples.
- In Science you should use accurate terms rather than leave a description in vague phrases. For instance, you may be asked how energy is transferred from the sun down through the earth's atmosphere. The correct answer will be "by radiation", rather than the vague "through the air".
- In many mathematical and scientific calculations the answer will have to be in some kind of unit. It is important not to put litres when it should be kilograms, or to leave an answer just as the number, when it should be specified as watts or joules.

SITTING EXAMS

- Some essay or short questions invite a definition of terms as part of the answer. For instance, a question in economics such as "What is the role of the government in a mixed economy?" is best answered by starting with a clear explanation of a mixed economy.
- Some Science questions are presented in everyday language because you are expected to be able to apply the ideas. However, such questions are a good opportunity to use the appropriate scientific terms.

Show your working

Many examiners' reports stress, almost sadly, how candidates could have gained themselves more marks, if only they had shown their working in any calculations. This point not only applies to maths, but also to some science or economics questions.

- You can still be given marks, even if your final answer is wrong, so long as you have shown your method, and it is correct.
- Correct answers do not bring the maximum marks possible when candidates have been asked to show their working and have failed to do so.
- Instructions will not necessarily be repeated for every question. Some exam papers have instructions on the front sheet like, for example, "Show all stages in any calculations and state the units".
- Sometimes the working will be the numbers involved, sometimes it will be that the rule or formula must be written out in full.
- If you are allowed a calculator in the exam, then you can check your answer. If your worked answer does not agree with the calculator one, then double-check your working. If you can see a mistake, correct it neatly. But, if you cannot see any mistakes, then do not cross out your working. You may have made the mistake on the calculator, but even if your

paper answer is wrong, you will get marks for a correct method.

Presentation

Examiners are not going to expect the standard of presentation that can be achieved in a project with far more time and resources at your disposal. However, they do expect reasonable standards of work, allowing for the constraints of a sit-down exam:

- Examiners will not persevere with illegible or scrappy exam papers. If they cannot read your correct answer, you will not get the marks.
- Essays should have a suitable structure. The basics are a beginning, middle and end. Your conclusion should pull the essay together and not be the time to introduce new points.
- Essays should be written in paragraphs, with decent spelling and punctuation.
- There are extra marks to be gained in GCSEs for a good standard in spelling, punctuation and appropriate use of technical terms (see page 137).
- Any maps, diagrams or graphs need to be neatly written and labelled.
- Any kind of illustration should be linked into what you have written. It should be made obvious to the examiner why you have included it.

Watch the time

It is important to pace yourself by keeping a careful eye on the time.

- There will only be so many marks for each section of the exam, so it will not help to put disproportionate amounts of time into your "best" question and give very skimpy answers to the others.
- If you are going to run out of time, then make a neat list of the

SITTING EXAMS

main points, along with the linked minor points and show as best you can, without writing it all out in full, where your answer would have taken you. You may gain some marks for your ideas and knowledge, even though you did not have time to write it all. However, be warned, offering notes is *not* an alternative to a properly written answer.
- If you have time, check back over the paper. If you have a lot of spare time, than you have almost certainly not written enough or have missed out a section of the paper. Look very carefully.
- If you see further points you would like to make in a completed answer, then add them neatly. For anything more than a few words, you will need to mark the position in your work with an asterisk and then make a note for the examiner such as "continued on page 10". On that page, make it clear that this is the extra material for, say, Question 3.

What is acceptable in exams and what is cheating?

- It is fine, of course, to have prepared as thoroughly as possible.
- It is always acceptable to have looked at previous papers
- There will be no problem in taking in study aids such as textbooks or calculators – **so long as explicit permission has been given for a particular exam or a particular child**. Permissions are specific and not general.
- Taking in hidden notes is cheating. It may result in disqualification, and not just from the exam in question.
- Looking at another pupil's work is cheating. In most exams, the desks will be far enough apart to make this kind of cheating very obvious.
- Getting hold of the current year's exam paper will always be cheating.
- It will be judged as cheating if non-permitted study aids are taken into the exam. Excuses such as, "It was fine in

> the economics exam, so I thought..." will be met with a stony stare.
> - Even when calculators are allowed, they are likely to have to be versions without substantial memories.

Exam and test results

The only fair expectation from parents is that their children and teenagers should do their best. The marks for tests and exams do matter and waiting for them can be a very worrying time, especially for public exams such as the GCSEs.

The best ways for parents to help are in the practical ways as outlined in the section on revision and sharing exam techniques. Some parents are tempted to offer financial incentives for good marks but this is unwise. You want your children and teenagers to work well because of their own personal satisfaction and because good work at school will support them into their adult life. The objective is not that they work hard for cash or a new bike. You also want them to be disappointed with poor marks and motivated, with your support, to do better next time. The disappointment needs to be over the poor mark and not the lost possessions that were promised "If..."

Children and teenagers should also be treated as individuals. It will only irritate or upset them to be compared with other brothers and sisters or friends. It is intensely discouraging to be told that "Your sister never had this kind of trouble with Spanish" or "Why can't you get marks like your friend Ben?" Any difficulties with a subject deserve help – not blunt and ultimately useless criticisms.

However, the children and teenagers who get high marks deserve acknowledgement of their hard work and their results. Parents need to show their appreciation, even if it is carefully expressed so as not to distress a brother or sister who has disap-

SITTING EXAMS

pointing results. Parents may need to step in on behalf of children with very good results, since relatives and friends of the family sometimes try to sweep these away. However you decide to reply, you should not let pass without comment remarks such as "Monica doesn't have to work, does she? She just sails through all these exams."

You need to be pleased when your child's hard work has paid off with good marks, and sympathetic if the final mark does not seem to reflect the effort that you know was made by your child or teenager. In public exams such as the GCSEs, and later the A levels or GNVQs, a low grade or a fail will have consequences. Parents can play a very important part in helping teenagers to pick up the pieces and plan what they will do, whether this involves re-sitting the exams or finding out if their preferred next step is still possible, perhaps with some changes.

CHAPTER SIX

GCSE coursework and exams

The GCSE programme

Methods of assessment

The days are gone when teenagers followed a course of study over a couple of years and then revised for timed, sit-down exams as the only judgement of their work over the years. Pupils now face a variety of methods of assessment and their final grade is made up of work over the two years as well as the results of their final exam.

Coursework

Some of the GCSE subjects are assessed partly through written coursework assignments that are given to pupils to complete and hand in by a certain deadline. The grade for the coursework contributes a percentage to the final GCSE grade. Coursework is more common with the arts subjects, such as Geography and English (more on page 115). Some subjects allow pupils to build up a portfolio of work and then to choose the best examples to submit towards their final GCSE grade. However, such a portfolio is not going to be so large that teenagers can risk skimping on pieces of coursework.

Investigations

Maths may be assessed by setting specific mathematical investigations that pupils take away and submit later. (See page 61 on this kind of work in earlier school years.)

Experiments

The science syllabus will include specific pieces of work that pupils carry out in the school laboratory. Much like the maths investigations, the particular project will be linked to the topic that pupils have been covering. Pupils know that they will be expected to carry out work on a particular day; it is not sprung on them without warning. They have to carry out and write up the work. Rather like the portfolio of coursework, pupils may be allowed to choose which reports of experiments they submit – selecting their best work. Again, there will not be so much manoeuvring room that teenagers can afford to discount some of the experiments.

Modular assessment

Some GCSE courses and more advanced exam syllabuses work on a modular basis. This means that as each topic is completed, pupils sit an exam on the work covered. Their results from this exam contribute towards their final grade. This section is now complete and pupils do not return to the material for the final exam.

Orals

The modern foreign languages will have an oral exam in which pupils take part in a conversation totally within that language. The person taking the oral will be an outsider to the school, but he or she will be asking questions from a range that teachers have practised with pupils.

Continued good work

Your teenager's ability is being assessed throughout the two years of the GCSE curriculum. The final exam is still very important, so the revision has to be taken seriously. However, a good standard of work throughout Years 10 and 11 will stand your teenager in good stead in two ways:

- She will be going into the final exam with a contribution already made towards her final grade.
- Teenagers agree that exam revision is much more straightforward, although still hard work, when they have good notes to revise from throughout the previous two years.

Be well informed

The pattern of assessment, including the percentage of coursework, is settling down in the National Curriculum. There have been changes from year to year and this is the reason to make sure that your information is up to date. The experience of teenagers – friends or older brothers and sisters – who passed through the process some years ago will not necessarily be an accurate measure of what is happening now.

Previous experiments of one hundred per cent coursework in some subjects have been abandoned for a more balanced mixture of assessment methods. All subjects must now have an exam at the end of the whole course, which is set by an external examining body. Syllabuses which are assessed on a modular system must still have a final exam which accounts for at least fifty per cent of the total marks. The highest proportion of total marks to be gained through coursework will be sixty or seventy per cent for subjects like Art or Physical Education. Modern foreign languages may not have any coursework, although there will be an oral exam.

GCSE COURSEWORK AND EXAMS

You and your teenager need to understand fully what kinds of assessment will emerge through the GCSE years and which of them are contributing to the final grade. For instance, teachers will still be giving class tests on French irregular verbs and end of topic reviews in Mathematics. These class assessments will help teacher and pupil to assess progress and to pick up on gaps in knowledge or understanding. But the marks are internal to the class and will not contribute to the end grade for the GCSE. Much depends, as always, on good communication between teachers and pupils and generally between home and school.

Tiering

In most GCSE subjects there are alternative papers, so all pupils do not sit an identical final exam. Teachers, supported by the relevant examining board, take responsibility for entering pupils for those exam papers which set realistic targets for their personal abilities. This decision has to be taken early on in the GCSE programme since it also affects the different possible kinds of coursework and their levels of difficulty. This system is called "tiering".

The process works slightly differently for different subjects. For instance, in Maths there are three overlapping tiers: one for pupils who are expected to gain a grade between A* and C, one for grades B to E and one for D to G. Some subjects just have two tiers. In subjects like Art and Music the final exam papers are designed to cover the full grade range and give pupils the scope to reply to the level that is within their own ability.

The result of tiering is that the groups of pupils who are entered for the less difficult papers will only be able to gain the top grade for that tier.

HELP YOUR CHILD WITH HOMEWORK AND EXAMS

> *Useful addresses*
>
> Your teenager's school should answer any questions that you have on the school curriculum. If you are having difficulty in getting information or you have more general questions, then the following organisations can help:
>
> - For England and Wales – the Schools Curriculum and Assessment Authority (SCAA), Newcombe House, 45 Notting Hill Gate, London W11 3JB. Tel: 0171 229 1234.
> - Northern Ireland Council for the Curriculum, Examinations and Assessment (CCEA), Beechhill House, 42 Beechhill Road, Belfast, BT8 4RS. Tel: 01232 704666.
> - The Scottish Consultative Council on the Curriculum (SCCC), Gardyne Road, Broughty Ferry, Dundee, DD5 1NY. Tel: 01382 455053.

Study for GCSEs

The pressure of work

Teachers, pupils and parents are all in agreement that there is a significant increase in the work pressure with the beginning of Year 10. If your teenager has established good habits of study in the earlier years of secondary school, then the difference will not seem so great. Your teenager will moan about the weight of homework and the coursework assignments but she will have skills of study that enable her to cope.

Teenagers who have not been well organised to date can get a very serious shock. It is not just that the amount of work increases, the standard expected is tougher. It is not impossible to motivate teenagers who suddenly realise that they have to work if they are to emerge with useful qualifications. But it is that much more difficult if they are trying to establish good study habits at the same time as coping with the increased work load.

Tougher marking systems

Teachers are very likely to mark work on a more stringent basis. This can be a shock to pupils who feel they are going backwards, since they are getting some lower grades than they experienced in previous years. Schools and teachers vary and the difference is more marked with some classes than others. Some schools shift from internal school marking systems to the GCSE patterns and pupils have to get used to what the grades now mean.

A great deal depends on how well teachers explain any changes and how they encourage pupils to judge their own work and the progress they are making. Internal school exams and the GCSE mock exams in the November of Year 11 may be marked strictly. Because pupils have not covered the complete GCSE course it can be impossible for them to get high marks. Teenagers need to have this explained, otherwise the results can be disheartening.

Coursework in GCSE

The significant change between your teenager's GCSE responsibilities and what you will recall from your school days is the reality of coursework. In some ways coursework is similar to project work that you may remember undertaking in some school subjects. The difference is that the grade for the coursework contributes directly to the final grade in that GCSE subject.

The programme for study in GCSE subjects now means that pupils cannot possibly coast through part of those two years and then make a mad dash in the last few months before exams. (It is questionable whether such a strategy was ever really possible, but the myth persists that some pupils used to manage reasonable grades in this way.) Coursework needs to be completed and submitted by the time deadlines. If pupils have not fulfilled the coursework requirements, then they are not entered for the examination part of the subject, and they will not be awarded any GCSE grade at all.

Deadlines

Schools set a series of deadlines for pupils throughout the two years in order to manage a reasonable workload. The coursework is probably not due to be given to the examining board until far closer to the GCSE exam period. So, if teenagers miss a school deadline through illness or an accident, then all is not lost. They can almost certainly submit the work later. However, they will, of course, have a heavy burden of work because other assignments will be following hard on the heels of the one that was disrupted for them.

Working to a deadline

Some teenagers (and adults) prefer to tackle a piece of work as soon as it is given out. In conversation, such teenagers explained to me that they disliked the sense of work hanging over them, they preferred to get down to the task almost straightaway. They welcomed help from their parents when they asked for it, but did not usually need reminding about the time deadline. Other teenagers explained that they needed the sense of pressure of seeing the deadline loom up before they started serious writing. These teenagers had not ignored the coursework up until then, they had spent the intervening time thinking over the topic, sometimes talking over the issues with their parents and collecting their notes together. Some admitted that they welcomed a reminder from their parents about the upcoming deadline – although their reaction might not always appear to be welcoming!

Some teenagers had a risky approach of leaving almost everything until the last moment. If your son or daughter takes this line then you may need to be very firm in your encouragement about getting down to work sooner rather than later. Ideally you want to dissuade her from this recipe for panic after her first coursework assignment shows how she is reacting. You may also know your teenager well enough to suspect that she may try to push off obligations until the very last moment.

If your teenager takes a sensible approach to coursework then she should not end up with more than one long piece of work to complete at the same time. She will, however, still have all her ordinary homework to undertake. When it comes to the actual writing, teenagers have to work in the way that suits them best. There is, however, an advantage to writing the draft of the first coursework assignment (rough or final) in one sitting because then your teenager has a reasonably accurate idea of how long such a piece of work will take her. Subsequent pieces of coursework will not all take the same amount of time but perhaps your teenager will understand that a good piece of work takes most of the day and not just an hour or so.

An honest approach to coursework

The whole point about coursework is that it should be pupils' own work. It is submitted for assessment of their individual progress and ability in the subject. However, the contents of a piece of coursework are not supposed to come solely from inside the teenager's head. It is entirely legitimate for teenagers to:

- Consult the notes they made as the topic was covered during lessons.
- Read around the topic and search out new information as appropriate for this piece of work. Some coursework needs further reading or practical research and some may not.
- Discuss their ideas with teachers, friends, parents, brothers and sisters, or experts on this topic.

Some kinds of coursework are undertaken with a group of other pupils. Perhaps a whole class will be part of a field study in Geography or several pupils will cooperate in gathering data for Economics or Child Development. Individuals' coursework must then show clearly their personal contribution to the larger project and the writing up must be the pupil's own work.

Coursework is a chance for teenagers to show that they have understood the topic and that they are able and motivated to take the material that bit further. The reading and discussion should be undertaken by the teenagers themselves as should final decisions about what is included in the coursework. Teenagers should do their own writing up, drawing of diagrams and tables and anything else that becomes part of what they submit.

What is cheating in coursework?

Coursework is supposed to be pupils' own work and they may be required to sign that they have understood this requirement when they hand in the work for assessment. Unfortunately coursework is open to abuse and this is harder for teachers to monitor than more traditional cheating in exams. However, teachers are not stupid and they are likely to spot differences in style or unlikely amounts of additional research in a pupil's assignment.

It will be regarded as cheating if pupils copy friends' coursework or allow friends to copy theirs. It would equally be seen as cheating if parents practically did the work for their teenagers. If cheating is discovered then pupils can be disqualified from that subject in their GCSE programme. Any such discovery will obviously make teachers very suspicious of any work in other subjects that could have been open to dishonesty. So one instance of cheating can cause teenagers serious trouble, even if that was genuinely the only time when they were tempted.

Parents understandably want their teenagers to get as good a grade as possible for their coursework. However, it is a very bad example to set to a son or daughter if parents take over the course-

GCSE COURSEWORK AND EXAMS

work. In the long term, teenagers need to gain in the confidence that they can organise themselves, collect information and work through drafts to a final piece of work that is their own best. They will not benefit educationally from learning that their mother is a tremendous speed reader of resource material or that their father drafts an impressive sentence. The teenagers are also losing the great opportunity to learn how to express themselves and present material well and clearly. They need these skills for other work such as exams.

I suspect that many more parents are too wary of helping because they are following an overly strict interpretation of "own work". Some parents seem to be concerned that even discussing a piece of coursework, or throwing out a few ideas with their teenagers will be seen by teachers as unacceptable help from home. Yet part of the way that teachers help is that they offer guidance on how coursework might be undertaken.

Helping with coursework – what is fair?

The following points are written to you as a parent but, of course, the same guidelines hold for anyone who might help teenagers – perhaps older brothers and sisters.

- **Do** talk through the possible ideas that could be included in a piece of coursework.
- **Don't** present your teenager with a list of ideas and tell her she should cover them.

- **Do** encourage your teenager to think about reading around the topic. (Not all coursework will need further reading.)
- **Don't** over-step the bounds to do this reading for your teenager.

- **Do** make helpful suggestions about how and where your teenager could find more information. You might

accompany her to a museum or explain how she could track down the telephone number to a useful organisation.
- **Don't** do the museum research or make the telephone calls for her.

- **Do** pass on anything of interest that you feel your teenager could use in this piece of coursework – for instance, a recent newspaper article.
- **Don't** insist that it has to be included.

- **Do** look at your teenager's plan for the coursework and make any comments.
- **Don't** do the plan for her, or insist on changes that you think would be an improvement.

- **Do** help your teenager (if she wants your help) by reading her first draft. It is fine to alert her to spellings that she should check, comment on layout and say if there are parts of the work where you cannot understand what she is communicating. You can discuss the draft with your teenager.
- **Don't** re-write it for her.

- **Do** remind him of good standards in presentation, such as "There don't seem to be any labels on this diagram" or "What happened to paragraph breaks?"
- **Don't** redraw diagrams for her or restructure her layout the way that you would write it.

- **Do** discuss the timing of coursework with your teenager – both in terms of the various steps and the final deadline. Some need more firm reminding than others!
- **Don't** take over the coursework because of your fear that your teenager is not managing her time effectively.

GCSE COURSEWORK AND EXAMS

Producing good coursework

Teachers are there to help pupils with their coursework. In no sense does all the responsibility rest with the teenagers themselves and their parents as home support.

Each piece of coursework should be given with a clear brief on the topic that the coursework should address and the deadline when it must be submitted. Sometimes teachers will give an interim deadline for the first draft and give pupils feedback on the material, which they can then re-draft and improve. Some coursework briefs include a list of key points that should be covered; pupils then have to find and organise the material to work through the points. In a similar way, pupils are given a clear layout of how they should write up the scientific experiments that they undertake within class time.

Follow the brief

Pupils should address the question, issue or focus that they have been given. For instance, if a piece of creative writing is supposed to be a story set in the future of how a hypothetical government controls children's education, then all those features must appear within the story. Pupils still have plenty of scope for their own imagination and personal twists to the events which unfold within the given framework.

Perhaps pupils can make a choice on their History coursework within the theme of "Conflict in the twentieth century". Discussion with teachers and the context of the coursework should explain further what is meant by "conflict". Pupils understand that this means fighting but not necessarily a formally declared war. They then have to decide which of the different armed conflicts they wish to choose, but they cannot research a completely different topic like political parties in the twentieth century.

Content

The length of a piece of coursework will vary but the longer ones should be about 1000–1500 words in length. Your teenager has the scope for a thorough coverage of a topic but she is not writing an enormous piece of work.

Good coverage of the topic

Pupils have, of course, to answer the question or issue that sets the whole framework for a certain piece of coursework. They have to cover all the key points. Sometimes teenagers should be presenting a balanced view of both sides of an argument, or detailing the advantages and disadvantages of a method or recent local development. Sometimes they will have to describe a chronological series of events and extract the main points from what happened.

Within the given framework pupils have to show that they have included the appropriate material. However, your teenager is likely to get a better grade if the finished coursework shows that she has made extra efforts to find fresh material or to present her ideas in an original way.

Presenting part of a study

In some GCSE subjects your teenager will be part of a team of pupils who have undertaken a study that would have been too time-consuming for one teenager. Each pupil in a team must be able to present a unique piece of work as her own coursework. The teacher should help in making sure that a larger project can be easily divided into individual pieces of work. For instance, a group of pupils might spend time in a playgroup for their study in Child Development but would make sure each member of the group was observing a different aspect of children's play.

GCSE COURSEWORK AND EXAMS

Ways for parents to help

Getting started

You are working here in a very similar way to the help you will have offered in earlier years. Suppose that your teenager has to undertake a piece of original creative writing in a short story format. She is stuck and wants your help. Try the following approach:

- Has your teacher given you any brief to follow? If so, what sort of framework has been set?
- Within that framework what would you like to write about? Or, if there are no limits, what would interest you?
- Get your teenager to make a list of possible topics on which to focus the writing.
- Do some topics throw up more ideas than others? Are there one or two that she would most like to write around?
- Get her to take one or two topics and note down a few ideas in rough on how that topic would develop. Or just talk it through with her, to encourage her to express the ideas.
- Which topic is emerging as the one that could lead to the best piece of work?
- Encourage your teenager to get a first draft down on paper. There is no way that a draft can be improved until she has written it down in the first place.

Health warning

The suggestion here is not that you ambush your son or daughter and insist on talking through every piece of work. Sometimes he may not want help and your best approach then is to confirm "I'm here if you change your mind."

HELP YOUR CHILD WITH HOMEWORK AND EXAMS

Talking around the topic

Suppose your daughter is writing up Geography coursework on the social advantages and disadvantages of a particular local shopping centre. She will have made visits with her class and should have plenty of material to draw on from class work notes and homework on the topic. However, she may welcome talking through with you the main ideas that she plans to work into her individual report. Your comments might follow a pattern along the lines of:

- I'm wondering if what you've just said is a mix of advantages and disadvantages.
- You seem to have a lot more disadvantages than advantages in your list. How do you think the shopping centre went ahead if so much seemed to be against it?
- I don't follow why that point is so important.
- That sounds interesting. Do you show that on your plan of the centre?
- That sounds like a direct quote from somebody – is it?
- I think there was an article in our local newspaper a couple of weeks ago. The library might help you there, or else you could contact the newspaper directly.

Of course, the points above are just *examples* – not suggestions to repeat word for word to your teenager. Your pattern needs to be one of listening carefully to what your teenager is telling you, showing interest and making comments that leave her able to make final decisions about her coursework. It must be her own work in the end.

In any kind of coursework, you want your teenager to have gained the habit of asking you for help before the time deadline is seriously close. She can then have time to think over possibilities before writing a rough and then final draft.

GCSE COURSEWORK AND EXAMS

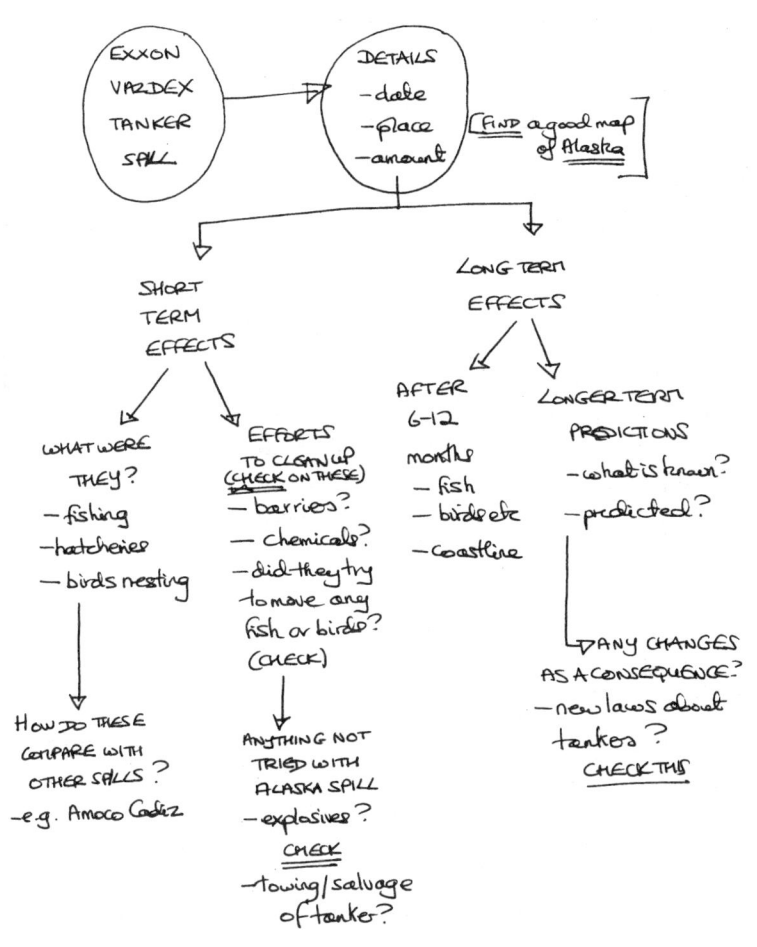

Figure 14 Using a diagram as a summary and forward plan

Listen to or read an early draft

You may be able to offer similar help when your teenager wants you to give an opinion on a first draft of a piece of coursework. It is important to be encouraging and express interest in the points that she has made. You might also suggest that she checks her spelling and paragraph breaks, if she seems to have overlooked these.

Comments about content can be more difficult because this is your teenager's coursework and not yours. Your style and the way that you would tackle a topic may not be the same as her and your preference may not be better for this work. The best approach is to keep to open-ended comments or questions that encourage your teenager to think, but which do not impose your view. For instance:

- What you say on the second page doesn't seem to fit with your very first point.
- I'm confused – can you run that bit past me again.
- You say the foreign policy was a disaster. Do you explain somewhere why?
- That's an interesting point. Is it backed up by the information you collected on the field trip?
- I think the whole piece could be stronger if you add a conclusion. Were you planning on that?

Using other resources

For some coursework pupils' previous work on a topic will be the source of most of what they need. However, in some types of coursework pupils will be expected to read more than just the course books that they have covered in class.

Teachers may make suggestions for further reading or expect that pupils know enough about the topic to browse the shelves of the school or local library. Reading around a subject or undertaking fact-finding on a topic could make your teenager's coursework stand out that much more. Pupils are not expected to undertake massive extra reading programmes but some additional work could help your teenager's final grade. In any kind of additional reading or research it will be important that your teenager makes good notes which will help her in the later writing (see page 42).

Good organisation and presentation

Coursework could, in theory, include all the relevant information but have it presented in such a random way that it would be impossible to understand what the coursework had covered and what sense had been made of all the material. This is one reason why pupils need to make a draft plan of their coursework and not simply fling down bits of information any old way.

Layout

The school will probably provide an official front sheet for your teenager's coursework, since all work will need the exam centre number and the syllabus title and number.

All coursework will need a title, your teenager's name and the date of completion. It may look neater to have a separate title page and then start the writing on the next sheet. If the coursework has a number of separate sections, then a simple contents list will look effective.

Most kinds of coursework will benefit from a proper structure of introduction, followed by separate sections or paragraphs. Most will also need a conclusion that draws together the key points but does not simply repeat, word for word, earlier bits of the work.

Getting the detail correct

Teenagers have the time to do proper plans, a rough draft and careful re-drafting. During this process they should take care over all the details of spelling, punctuation, grammar, use of illustrations and different resources. Look at Chapters 2 and 3 for thorough coverage of all these points. Extra marks are available in GCSE coursework for good spelling, punctuation and proper use of technical terms (see page 137).

HELP YOUR CHILD WITH HOMEWORK AND EXAMS

Fixing the material together

The sheets of paper should be fixed together in a neat way but examiners are not looking for fancy binding systems. The preference is for a simple system of sheets fixed in order and placed in a folder or binder. Pages should be numbered. Different kinds of work will need slightly different kinds of presentation, but none will look good as a collection of loose sheets.

The marking of coursework

Interim feedback from teachers

Some teachers may take in your teenager's draft coursework assignment and make some suggestions for improvement. Depending on their experience, teenagers may initially find this kind of feedback difficult. They may feel that they have finished that piece of work and given it in, so why do they have to go through it again. Depending on how constructively the teacher offers comments, teenagers may also have a sense of being criticised rather than helped.

Parents can probably help at home, especially if you have offered support in the past. You may need to edge your teenager towards accepting the whole idea of fine-tuning a piece of work and in finding a sense of satisfaction as a subsequent draft is a real improvement on the earlier one.

Final marking

The GCSE coursework is initially marked by the teachers in your teenager's school. However, an external moderator studies the coursework of all schools to ensure that standards are consistent across schools. Any moderator who judges that a teacher's standards are too generous, or too strict, is empowered to adjust the marks. So, it is unlikely that your teenager's teachers will tell pupils of the marks gained in their coursework, once it has finally been handed in. This move would be unfair to pupils, since the moderator might later change the marks.

Revision for GCSEs

Everything no longer depends solely on the final exams, but they are still very important. Coursework may deliver up to fifty or sixty per cent of the final grade in some subjects but the percentage is much less in others. No pupil will manage to get a good overall grade by concentrating on the coursework and ignoring the exams.

Building on previous experience

All the practical advice offered in Chapters 4 and 5 is equally relevant to sitting the GCSE exams. Teenagers who have learned how to revise and how to approach exams in their earlier years will be well prepared. Yet, there is no doubt that the GCSE exams can feel more daunting than any previous exams, because their consequences are more serious. The final grade is determining a national qualification and one that will stay with your teenager for life. Future employers or the interview boards of colleges will not be asking how he did in his end of Year 8 school exams. They will want to know how many GCSEs he has and the grades.

Organising for GCSE revision

Teachers should be giving pupils advice about revision but schools vary in what they offer:

- Some issue revision lists to guide teenagers through all the topics that have been covered, and so should be revised.
- Some teachers run revision classes in the last weeks before the exams start and these sessions can be very useful for your teenager to ask about topics or methods that are still puzzling her.

HELP YOUR CHILD WITH HOMEWORK AND EXAMS

- Some teachers provide time for revision but leave the work mainly up to the pupils.
- Schools also vary in when they no longer require pupils to attend school every day. Some let pupils study at home for some time before the beginning of the exam period, whereas others expect full attendance until the first exam starts.

A revision timetable

Your teenager needs some plan to order her work since she has a lot of subjects to cover. A revision timetable will help her pace herself, ensure coverage of all the topics and give her some reassurance of progress through the task of revision. Teenagers vary (as do adults) in the level and kind of structure that they find genuinely helpful. However, no teenager will get by with a plan that boils down to "I'll do what I can when I can fit it in".

Some study guides recommend a complex layout that includes hour by hour planning in a day, but I have never known a teenager who benefits from this level of detail. There is also a risk that drawing up the revision timetable can become more important that getting down to the actual work of revision. A more detailed version of the timetable on page 82 should work well.

Teenagers have a lot of material to cover and it can encourage them to keep track of their progress by ticking off topics they have covered. They also need to monitor how well they are moving through all the subjects.

Pattern of working

Teenagers also vary over what time of the day they prefer to work. Their preferred schedule might not be what you would choose if you had this pressure of work, but it is important to respect your teenager's way of working and you should have experience now on how well this works in practice.

Some teenagers are definitely morning people and prefer to get up promptly, perhaps even before the rest of the family, and do most of their serious work before lunch. They may then be ready for a well-earned break and go out to see friends. Other teenagers are natural night owls and do their best work from late afternoon onwards, perhaps having slept late in the morning. As a parent, your responsibility is to keep any eye on the fact that your teenager does work and not to insist that the work follows a schedule that would make sense to you.

Organising the material

There is no doubt that good notes will make your teenager's revision task much easier. But, she will still have to remind herself where all the material is placed within her books and then start to refresh her memory.

- Some teenagers find it useful to organise a separate revision folder in which they place their summaries of key information, methods in Maths or Science, definitions or list of phrases for their foreign language.
- Not all teenagers want to organise themselves with a separate folder and prefer to make summary notes of all the key topics.
- A list of headings or ideas organised as a diagram (see page 79) can help teenagers to extract the main points from a topic. This method can also provide the best notes for the "last minute" revision of the day before the exam.
- Teachers should tell your teenager what equipment they will be allowed to take into each exam. If any texts are allowed for literature, your teenager will still need to revise that subject. There will not be time in the exam to find parts of a book or play that he does not know well.

Revision books

It is possible to obtain revision books on most of the GCSE subjects. Both Letts and Longman publish a series. You might buy these or borrow them from your local library. Some teenagers find revision books very helpful, especially for some subjects. For example, the summaries in History are useful to order the information that your teenager is revising. A Science book may have concise definitions that are easier to see and learn than the material in your teenager's workbook. Some revision workbooks are helpful as teenagers work out how to structure information in the way that examiners prefer.

Helping your teenager

You have no choice but to trust your teenager to a great extent. You will not help by cross-questioning her on a regular basis. Use many of the ways that you supported her in earlier years:

- The most likely direct help that your teenager will request will be to test her knowledge when she feels she has learned a topic. With the book in front of you, you might be testing her foreign language vocabulary, definitions in Science or key issues in a History topic.
- Remind your teenager about work if the revision timetable seems to be slipping. Your reminder may not be met with a happy smile but it needs to be made as courteously as possible.
- Your teenager may welcome your help in dealing with friends who want to get together when your son or daughter needs to work.
- Make sure that your teenager is eating well. You may need to be more flexible about mealtimes or at least make sure that she eats her meal, perhaps re-heated, when she emerges. You will also help by stocking up the fridge with a good store of reasonably nutritious snacking food and drinks.

Revising with friends?

Some teenagers have no doubt that they work better on their own and want to revise in solitude. Others like company and may propose that they go round to a friend's house to revise or that the friend should join them in your house. Some teenagers will have girl- or boyfriends and may wish to revise in each other's company.

Parents can make a decision on this issue only in the light of what they already know about their teenager's habits and from trying out the proposal on an experimental, "Let's see how you manage" basis.

Some friends genuinely support each other's concentration, while others may be a hopeless distraction. A teenage couple who are serious about study may work well together, at least for some of the revision time. An additional point to bear in mind is that they may be badly distracted by missing each other, if solitary study is imposed by the two families. On the other hand, another couple may simply be plotting to spend more time together shut in one of their bedrooms. You have to make a judgement from your knowledge of your own teenager.

Experience of exam papers

Pupils should not be surprised or shocked by the structure of any exam paper because their teachers should have given them plenty of experience in the kinds of questions that they will be asked.

Practice with previous papers

Teachers should give pupils practice with exam questions from previous papers and the school is responsible for the full-scale practice of the GCSE mock exams. These exams, run under full exam conditions, will happen in November of Year 11.

GCSE exam papers are very clearly laid out, with all the relevant instructions. Teenagers just have to make sure they read them. The papers themselves also give the number of marks that can be gained from each question, so teenagers are effectively guided not to spend an extraordinary amount of time on a question that will only deliver a few marks. The number of blank lines provided for the answer is also some indication of the length of reply that is expected with the short-answer questions.

Sending off for papers at home

Some parents send off for the exam papers for their teenagers. You need to know which examining group is setting the paper for your teenager's school. You then contact the relevant board (see the box below), ask for the publications department and they will send you a catalogue and order form.

Copies of past exam papers will be the most relevant for home study but you can order other material as well. You can purchase a copy of the exam syllabus for any subject. This can be useful if your teenager is having difficulty in grasping the overall framework of the subject. The syllabus layout can be one way to organise for revision. Examiners' reports are available for some of the previous years' exams and sometimes other material as well, such as the role cards for foreign language work.

GCSE Examination Boards

England and Wales:

- Midland Examining Group (MEG), 1 Hills Road, Cambridge CB1 2EU. Tel: 01223 553311.
- Northern Examining Association Board (NEAB), Devas Street, Manchester M15 6EX. Tel: 0161 9531180.
- Southern Examining Group (SEG), Stag Hill House, Guildford GU2 5XJ. Tel: 01483 506506.
- University of London Examinations and Assessment Council (ULEAC), 32 Russell Square, London WC1B 5DN. Tel: 0171 3314000.

- Welsh Joint Education Committee (WJEC), 245 Western Avenue, Cardiff CF5 2YX. Tel: 01222 561231.

Northern Ireland:

Northern Ireland Council for the Curriculum, Examinations and Assessment (CCEA), Beechhill House, 42 Beechhill Road, Belfast BT8 4RS. Tel: 01232 704666.

Scotland:

Scottish Examining Board (SEB), Ironmills Road, Dalkeith, Midlothian EH22 1LE. Tel: 0131 6636601.

You need to be guided by your teenager as to the way that she wants to use previous exam papers at home – and some teenagers feel that they get enough practice at school. If your teenager's school is overlooking this important form of preparation, then do send off for papers yourself. Home practice may take the form of writing out whole answers when these are relatively short. The longer essay-type questions might be practised by drafting a detailed plan for an answer.

Predicting this year's paper?

Some pupils try to predict the sort of questions that will be asked for their exam. They develop theories such as "Gladstone's foreign policy has come up three times in the last five years, so it probably won't come up this year" or "There's always something about velocity in Science."

The point of trying to predict is usually to reduce the revision job by concentrating on fewer topics. This is a very risky approach and not to be recommended. The people who develop the exam papers are not going to be completely predictable and topics may come up again or with a different angle.

The GCSE exam period

Internal school exams may be concentrated into one or two weeks, but there are many more potential GCSE subjects than a single school can offer. Consequently, the entire spread of all the GCSE exams will be a matter of weeks. Your teenager is likely to have days in between exams. This time may be useful for last-minute revision of notes but it should not be seen as the only time to do revision. There is no way that your teenager will fit it all in.

The timetable for the GCSEs is drawn up well in advance. Since pupils may be sitting exams from more than one board, all the examining groups have to work together to produce a timetable in which there are no clashes. So the school and therefore your teenager should have a full timetable, in which she can highlight her exams in plenty of time before the very first one.

Get there!

The final detail of preparation for the GCSEs, or any public exam, is to get there, with the right equipment for each exam. Schools are very likely to require pupils only to be in school for their own exams once the examination period starts. The responsibility for ensuring that pupils get into the right location on time rests with the teenagers themselves and with their parents. Apparently a proportion of pupils fail exams solely because they never turned up on the day. Some were ill, of course, but at least some got confused over which day, or part of the day they were due to sit the exam.

It may seem very obvious, but make sure that your teenager has an accurate timetable for the whole GCSE exam period and that it is fixed up somewhere prominent. If your teenager is prone to losing things, it might be worth making a copy for yourself and pinning it up somewhere where you can check. She needs to know exactly when, and if necessary, where, each exam is taking place and make sure that she gets out of the house on time.

GCSE COURSEWORK AND EXAMS

Even if your teenager is running late and will inevitably miss the start of the exam, it is crucial still to go. Exam invigilators can usually allow latecomers to join the exam up to a given time into the exam sitting. The teenagers are not, of course, given extra time to compensate for their lateness.

Completing the exams

All the practical advice given in Chapter 5 is applicable for the different kinds of exams in the range of GCSE subjects. Crucial issues such as management of time, reading the questions properly and planning out an essay-type answer all hold for these public exams as much as for all the internal school exams of previous years. Here are a few additional points:

Spelling, punctuation and grammar

The Schools Curriculum and Assessment Authority (SCAA) has developed criteria for the marking of all subjects in which pupils are required to write in sentences. These criteria do not apply to the multiple choice or practical tests.

Five per cent of the marks of each written exam paper are allocated to quality of spelling, punctuation, grammar and appropriate use of specialist terms for the subject. Care in these aspects will therefore affect pupils' final marks and could make the difference between one grade and another. Marks are allocated on the same basis for the coursework required in different subjects. The pattern is:

- At the "threshold performance" candidates can gain one extra mark for reasonably accurate spelling, punctuation and use of the rules of grammar.
- "Intermediate performance" gains two to three marks, for which candidates have to be accurate in the above. They also have to use some specialist terms – correctly.
- "High performance" gains four to five marks, and for this can-

didates have to show almost faultless spelling, punctuation and grammar. Their use of words and phrases, including specialist terms, has to be precise and well applied.

Acceptable exam aids

Teachers should give pupils very clear instructions as to what, if any, aids they can take into the exam. Teenagers have, of course, to take in their own pens, pencils, rubbers and any special items such as mathematical protractors or a pair of compasses.

In most instances, pupils will not be allowed to take dictionaries or any other kind of spelling aid into the exam, nor will they be allowed bilingual dictionaries for foreign languages. They *may* be allowed a calculator but your teenager must be sure whether this is permitted or not. More powerful calculators with memories are not allowed. Teachers and examiners realised that the memories could be programmed to hold information that pupils are supposed to have memorised.

There are special arrangements that can be made for pupils with learning disabilities such as dyslexia. However, these will not be in force for your teenager unless her difficulty has been previously assessed and discussed with the school. It will be too late to ask for special treatment as the deadlines loom for coursework or at the start of the exam period.

A good standard of work

All the practical points made in Chapter 5 still hold for the GCSE exams. Your teenager will be well prepared if she has good exam habits such as reading the question properly, managing her time, planning out an essay answer and showing her working neatly in a calculation or formula problem.

The seriousness of the exams may mean that your teenager needs to calm herself down and take a few deep breaths before starting. She may also need to have avoided the wind-up that can result from milling about with others as they wait for the exam to start. It is best to side-step any friends who are going on at length about "I didn't revise enough!" or "Do think they'll be a question on...?"

The grading system

The exam is graded from A through to G. Grades from A to C are equivalent to the old O level pass grades of A, B and C, which is the reason that schools give their results for the proportion of A–C grades. A* is outstanding, the best possible grade in the subject. U grade means unclassified and is a fail.

The number of passes in GCSEs will matter for your teenager since these qualifications are relevant to further education and for entry into many jobs. Some advanced courses (GNVQ and A level) and some jobs may require a particular grade of pass in certain subjects.

The results

It can be a tense time for teenagers and their parents as they wait over the summer for the GCSE results. It will be very disappointing for your teenager if she does not get enough GCSEs for her chosen course of action or not at a high enough grade. Your support may be important in encouraging her to try again, since it is possible to re-sit GCSEs. Consider organising some extra tuition for your teenager to give her the best chance possible next time around.

If your teenager does as well, or even better, than she hoped then it is a time for celebration. Young people deserve some rest because the next stage of their life, whether it is further education or job hunting, will come along very quickly indeed.

Index

A
A levels 109

C
cheating 5, 107, 118
coursework 20, 42
checking work 40–2, 125
computers 18–22, 29
confidence 22–6
coursework in GCSE 20, 42, 94, 115–29
creative writing 48

D
deadlines
 coursework for GCSE 110, 116
 homework 8, 12
design technology 66–70
diagrams 44–6, 79, 125
dictionary 15, 138

difficulties with a subject 71–3
dyslexia 32, 57, 138

E
encouragement 22–6, 108
entrance exams 88
essays 35–40, 52, 102
exams
 different types of questions 97–103
 entrance exams 88
 examining boards 134–5
 GCSEs 20, 42, 73, 91, 129–36
 practice on past papers 88, 133–5
 revision 10, 42, 80–6, 129–36
 SATs 10, 86, 87, 95
 technique 87, 93–108

INDEX

F
family activities 18, 90
foreign languages
   confusions with grammar 53
   memorising 53, 74, 83
   orals 54, 88, 111, 112
friends
   helping with homework 11, 27, 73
   revising with 132

G
GCSEs
   coursework 20, 42
   exams 108, 129–36
   examining boards 134–5
grading system
   methods of assessment 110–12
   tiering 113
GNVQs 109
grammar
   foreign languages and 53

H
homework
   charters 8
   diary 8, 12
   getting organised for 10–14
   illustrations in 32
   timetable 8

I
information technology 20

L
legibility 31, 42
libraries 16

M
making notes 42–3
marks
   homework 8
   GCSE coursework and exam 115, 128, 137
maths
   boys versus girls 65
   investigations 61–3, 111
   talking through problems 56–60
memorising techniques 75–9
mistakes
   helping with children's 22–3
   neatness in correcting 33
music
   as background 32
   as a subject 113

N
neatness 31, 33
Northern Ireland and education 114

O
orals
   foreign languages 54, 88
   on coursework 88–9

P
paragraphs 41

parts of speech   53
planning work   35, 48, 52, 102, 130
positive criticism   22–3
presentation of written work   28–35, 106, 127
private tutor   72
punctuation   41, 46, 137

Q
quotations   43

R
reading
  for homework   15–18, 117, 126
  for pleasure   14
  making notes from   42–3, 85, 112
  out loud to check work   41, 125
reference books   15–16
report from school   9
results of tests and exams   108, 139
revision   80–6
rough drafts   28, 127

S
SATs   10, 86, 87, 95
science
  boys versus girls   65
  experiments   34, 64, 111
  GCSEs   111
Scotland and education   114
speaking in class   70
special educational needs   32, 57, 138
spelling   22, 46, 75, 137
social life
  exam revision and   90
  homework and   10–11
styles of writing   38, 48

T
teachers
  help from   29, 72, 81, 86, 95, 101, 117, 122, 123
  relationship with parents   7, 8–10
tests in class   74–80, 113
thesaurus   15
tiering   113
television   13, 17, 32
time, managing   10–14, 106, 116–17
timetable   8, 11–12, 81, 130
trust   132

W
word processing   19, 20–2, 29
workbooks   58, 59, 72, 86, 131

Positive Parenting

Positive parenting is a series of handbooks primarily written for parents, in a clear, accessible style, giving practical information, sound advice and sources of specialist and general help. Based on the authors' extensive professional and personal experience, they cover a wide range of topics and provide an invaluable source of encouragement and information to all who are involved in child care in the home and in the community.

Other books in this series include:

Talking and your child by Clare Shaw – a guide outlining the details of how speech and language develops from birth to age 11 and how parents can help with the process.

Your child from 5–11 by Jennie and Lance Lindon – a guide showing parents how they can help their children through these crucial early years, stressing the contribution a caring family can make to the emotional, physical and intellectual development of the child.

Help your child through school by Jennie and Lance Lindon – a guide which looks at the school years from the perspective of the family, showing how parents can help their children to get the most out of their years at primary school and how to ease the transition into secondary education.

Help your child with maths by Sue Atkinson – a comprehensive guide to show parents how they can help develop their children's mathematical awareness and confidence from babyhood through the primary years and into secondary school.

Help your child with reading and writing by Lesley Clark – a guide which describes the stages children go through when learning to read and write and shows parents how they can encourage and enjoy their children's early development in these vital areas.

Help your child with a foreign language by Opal Dunn – written for all parents, including those who do not speak a foreign language, this guide examines the right time to start teaching a child a foreign language, how to begin, and how to progress to fluency.

Prepare your child for school by Clare Shaw – a very practical guide for parents whose children are about to start school.

Teenagers in the family by Debi Roker and John Coleman of the Trust for Adolescence covers all the major issues that parents face as their children pass through the turbulent teenage years, such as rules and regulations, setting boundaries, communication, decision making, risky behaviour, health issues, and problems at school.

Teenagers and sexuality by John Coleman of the Trust for Adolescence gives practical advice for parents who are finding it difficult to talk to their teenagers about sex and who need help to understand, and deal with, their teenagers' emerging sexuality.